# THE POWER WE POSSESS

# THE POWER WE POSSESS

*Understanding the Power of Your Vote and the Need for the Political Evolution of the Black Electorate*

DR. JOHNNIE CORDERO

BES Publishing Company

# CONTENTS

# Dedication

This book is dedicated to the memory of Brandon T. Harris, my brother, student, teacher, and friend whose life, more than his untimely death, from Sickle Cell taught me the joy of life contemplating death. He never once complained about his lot in life but by his living example demonstrated his strength, endurance, and wisdom far beyond his years. Thank you, my brother I will never forget you recognizing as our ancestors did, that we do not really die until the last person who remembers us dies. I will keep you alive for the rest of my days and beyond because I will always sing your praises to everyone I meet. Until we meet again. *Hetep.*

# Acknowledgements

I would be remiss if I failed to acknowledge the assistance of Michael Bailey journalist, friend, founder, and curator of the Minority Eye Columbia's foremost minority news and information platform who took time from his busy schedule to review the manuscript for this book and who provided valuable suggestions. The subtitle of this book was one of his suggestions. Thank you, my friend. Couldn't have done it without you.

# Introduction

"The most common way people give up their power
is by thinking they don't have any." Alice Walker

*THE POWER WE POSSESS: Understanding the
Power of Your Vote and the Need for the Political Evolution of Black Voters,* seeks to answer a simple yet profound
question.

- **The Question:** Why African Americans, now 157
  years since the passage of the 13th Amendment with an
  estimated population of 48 million and an estimated
  gross domestic product (GDP) of $1.2 trillion, have
  not attained political power in America at least proportionate to our numbers in the population?
- **The Answer:** The answer lies in (1) our collective
  failure to recognize the importance of politics in the
  quest for power *and* (2) our collective failure to develop *effective* political strategies and tactics utilizing a
  military mindset.

The key word here is *effective*. We must recognize at
the outset, to paraphrase Albert Einstein, *that doing the
same thing over and over expecting different results is at best
counterproductive and at worst insane.* We have protested and

marched and rallied and created organizations and protested and marched some more. But we have not secured power proportionate to our numbers nor have we accumulated wealth reflective of our forced contribution to the building of this country in uncompensated labor and the effect of discriminatory government policies thereafter.

In order to answer the question and provide solutions in the form of strategies and tactics to reverse our collective circumstances going forward we will explore the definitions of and symbiotic relationship between power, politics, and leadership. We will answer the question of what we can do *now* to effect substantive, measurable change in one generation.

The understanding of power and the power process is necessary because it is the power that drives all other forces; without it, we will forever be second-class citizens or worse, in a country that we helped build.

In short, we must recognize that the accomplishment of any objective is virtually impossible without power as its motive force. We require power to protect and defend our families and our heritage. We require power to survive and prosper. We require power to secure our possessions. Without power, we cannot effectively or assuredly accomplish any of these things. This may explain why we often appear to act against our own best interests and find it difficult to work together against our common enemy. It follows that the lack of power in a real sense impedes meaningful cooperation and nation-building as well.

## CHAPTER ONE

# This is War!

"The supreme art of war is to subdue the enemy without fighting." Sun Tzu

## *Introduction*

Warfare begins and ends with confusion and deception. In armed conflict, confusion is the goal of the primary military tactic of cutting off the head of the enemy so that its body will die. This tactic requires the identification and elimination of the leader so that the troops will scatter in confusion having lost their brain, or more accurately, their ability to think under the pressure of battle. The problem with this tactic is that it is a bloody and inefficient way to confuse the thought processes of the enemy. It also runs the risk of transforming the leader into a martyr thereby making her greater in death than she was in life. The efficiency of the technique lies only in the fact that once armed hostilities have begun it is the quickest way to accomplish the goal.

Psychological warfare can be as deadly and accurate as a bullet. It can also be more effective. It's primary effectiveness lies in the fact that its theater of operation is not a battlefield but the confines of the human mind. Its armaments, though as devastating as a well-placed bomb, are not explosive or incendiary devices. It's soldiers, highly trained mercenaries all, do not wear battle fatigues unless a double-breasted Armani can be defined as uniform. The planners and engineers of psychological warfare prosecute the war on Madison Avenue, in Hollywood, and for the Central Intelligence Agency and now by Facebook and Tik Tok, Twitter, and Instagram. They may be executive producers, directors, advertising executives, operations analysts, or deep-cover operatives. No matter what guise they assume the goal is the same: *control the enemy by controlling what he thinks, control what he thinks by controlling the information he receives.*

Psychological warfare is the use of mental means to influence and confuse the thinking and morale of the enemy. In this context, morale is defined as a condition that comprises courage, discipline, confidence, enthusiasm, and willingness to endure hardship for a cause. Without it all of these otherwise immediately apparent and immediately obtainable goals are impossible. Clearly, a person who is confused about any or all of the components of morale is unlikely to be able to develop the stuff of which warriors are made. They will never fight, join the battle or counsel others to do so. They have been effectively defeated by the subtle tactic of psychological warfare.

Psychological warfare is admittedly long-term, but it is also a more efficient way to defeat the enemy by confusion. When psychological warfare is waged against the enemy from his childhood it has the predictable effect of decreasing the possibility that they will ever contemplate, let alone cultivate, the idea of revolution as a remedy for injustice. *The ability to control or influence the thinking of the enemy is as important as the soldier and his gun.*

The point of all of this is that we have yet to recognize, collectively, that we are at war. A centuries-long war has been waged against us and our ancestors and everyone seems to know it but us. But we are not here talking about a war of weapons although it was superior weapons that made the kidnap and enslavement of millions of our ancestors possible. We are now talking about a war of wits - a war for the minds of our people. In this war, we are confronted with the baggage of past beliefs that serve only to confuse our understanding of the present. As George Orwell said in his classic 1984 "Who controls the past controls the future. Who controls the present controls the past."

In order to effectively defend ourselves at this stage of the war we must as quickly as possible develop strategies and tactics to counteract the enemy assault. In order to do that we must develop a military mindset. By military mindset, I mean the development and use of strategic and tactical thinking techniques employed by the military in prosecuting war but applied to our quest for power proportionality. In short, *we must start thinking like generals in the midst of a psychological (mind) war.*

## CHAPTER TWO

# The Military Mindset

There are those in the African American Community who earnestly, but mistakenly still believe that the people who enslaved us will somehow free us from the lingering effects of that slavery. This fundamentally illogical and catastrophically dangerous belief is the result of generations of indoctrination at the hands of nefarious slave masters, white supremacists and perhaps worst of all our parents who continued to spoon feed us the belief systems that continue to keep us mentally enslaved long after the real shackles have been removed. This love your neighbor, God's got a plan, pie in the sky philosophy has not only misled us but has also prevented us from developing the military mindset without which we will be forever subject to the whims and caprices of people who have demonstrated their ill-will toward us in every conceivable way for centuries. You cannot love your enemy and fight your enemy at the same time. For the simple fact that in order to love your enemy you have to see him as a friend or at least not an enemy. Therein lies the problem. The remedy is the development of a Military Mindset.

The military mindset demands first and foremost the existence and identification of the enemy. No enemy, no war. If you cannot identify who or what is the enemy, how can you defeat them? The answer is you can't. Your enemy is not necessarily the person who did you wrong today. The determination of who the enemy is cannot turn on who smiles at you or agrees with you today or hates you today for that matter. Our ancestors decided millennia ago that the enemy was best understood as *anyone who was not of your tribe or who did not march under your standard.* In short, either you are with us or against us. No in between. Seems harsh - maybe - but one thing is certain it was not until we abandoned that rule that our real troubles began.

The second thing that the military mindset demands is that we remember the root of the word war means *to bring into confusion.* Now on to psychological (mind) warfare.

## CHAPTER THREE

# Psychological Warfare

Clearly, we are at war. Yet unbelievably our response has been to appeal to the conscience of those who have demonstrated beyond doubt that they have no conscience. Our war cry in response to a history of atrocities has been to "forgive them for they no not what they do." Nonsense. They know good and damn well what they have done. Because they did it premeditatedly with malice aforethought to use a legal term. They cannot now, at this late date, claim clean hands.

Over the years I have asked the following question of friends and acquaintances both male and female who have had military training. The question I asked them was "If you viewed the situation confronting our people historically and presently, as a military campaign against a well-armed enemy would you recommend the plan used to date by our leaders?" The answer was always a resounding no and often a resounding hell no! I never asked any of them to tell me how a military plan would be different because it was obvious to me that difference lay not so much in the ultimate plan as in the initial approach. That is, would they be planning to make love or war?

Admittedly, I have no military training. Despite that, it seems obvious to me that if we are truly at war (we are) we must recognize that fact and start thinking like generals. That is we must develop a *military mindset*. It is my understanding that a general's job is to develop strategies and tactics to win the war (defeat the enemy) as quickly as possible. And that a general works at the strategic, operational, and political level of war.

With this in mind, I concluded who better to inform our strategy than the military and who better than the United States Marines. The following information is excerpted from the Tactical Planning Student Handbook[7] used by the United States Marine Corps in its Basic Officer Course.

### The Tactical Thought Process

1. The Tactical Thought Process, . . . applies analysis to the development of a *tactically sound plan* that ultimately counters the enemy's course of action.
2. The process begins with a detailed analysis of the situation, or Estimate of the Situation.
3. Using the details of that estimate, the leader determines the Enemy's Most Likely Course Of Action (EML-COA).
4. Identifies: the center of gravity of the enemy; the enemy's critical vulnerability or gap associated with the identified center of gravity; and the best way to

strike this vulnerability known as the Exploitation Plan (EXP)

5. The objective of an analysis of the enemy situation is to understand how the enemy will use each element of his combat power. Its development comes from many sources including enemy doctrine, current enemy activities indicated in higher order, adjacent units that have previously operated in the area, or the intelligence section. The commander must know what information is valid from each of these sources regarding their specific enemy and the relationship they have with a higher or adjacent enemy.

6. The enemy has several surfaces, but we must commit our focus to one center of gravity

7. Remember, the center of gravity is the element or capability that allows the enemy to accomplish your prediction of their SOM (EMLCOA)

## *The Tactically Sound Plan*

The tactically sound plan is not necessarily a winning plan. It is a plan that is sound based on the *current* circumstances. In war, conditions change daily and the constant updating of reconnaissance in real time is absolutely necessary. It follows that the plan must be one that takes into consideration as many variables as possible and is based on current reconnaissance that is continually updated in real-time. It also follows that a plan developed in the 1960s may not be a tactically sound plan today. In short, *a war plan cannot be static.*

It also follows that in war you must, as a primary objective, determine who or what the enemy is. This is important. For far too long we have failed to recognize not only that we are at war but also who or what we are at war with. More precisely, who or what is the real enemy?

*Let us be clear here.* The enemy is not white people individually or collectively. They are merely the secondary beneficiaries of the enemy's actions. Nor is the enemy *racism*. That someone doesn't like me because of the color of my skin is frankly irrelevant to me. First, I know that there is only one race - the human race. Second, I don't care. The myth of race was created to justify the enslavement of Africans. It was and remains a smokescreen, subterfuge, obfuscation - *psychological warfare but warfare nonetheless.* So before we go on let's settle once and for all who/what is the enemy against which we must fight. It is not a person but an ideology called *white supremacy*.

## Digression: White Supremacy Defined

*The real enemy against which we must do battle is the political, economic, and cultural ideology known as white supremacy.* It is an all-encompassing strategy designed to ensure that certain people rule the world in perpetuity. *It is made up of an intricate series of interlocking laws, policies, treaties, and judicial opinions based on custom and usage and backed by the ever-present threat of massive violent force.*

But the term white supremacy is itself intentionally misleading no doubt to cause confusion. It is intentionally misleading because it was developed as " . . . a social system based on or perpetuating the political, economic, and cultural dominance of white people."[8] It is not a statement that white people are superior, although many of these people may have believed it and still believe so, it is the *intended goal of the political, economic, and cultural ideology.*

Although the first attested appearance of the term is from 1868 as part of the title of the book "*White Supremacy and Negro Subordination,*"[9] it is clear that the concept existed long before 1868. In 1684, François Bernier, a French physician published the first work that classified humanity by race.[10] He concluded Europeans are the norm from which other races "deviated".

The bottom line is that it was called white supremacy because those who created it were greedy white males who adopted racism to justify their real motivation. The heart of this pernicious ideology and its sole driving force is and has always been - *greed.*

Greed is a selfish, excessive desire for more of something (such as money) than is needed.[11] *That is more than one's fair share.* Because of this selfish desire, these men created the ideology of white supremacy. Today, however, it is not only white men, it is greedy people who have learned to use the strategy of white supremacy to their advantage whether they are white or not.

Historically and presently this nefarious ideology has been used to subjugate, exploit and enslave much of the world and now as a result controls most of the wealth of the world. Now that we have identified the enemy and defined white supremacy let us move on to a detailed analysis of the situation confronting us.

*Detailed Analysis of the Situation*

***"The art of war teaches us to rely not on the likelihood of the enemy's not coming, but on our own readiness to receive him;not on the chance of his not attacking, but rather on the fact that we have made our position unassailable." Sun Tzu***

The development of the tactically sound plan begins with a detailed analysis zof our situation presently and against the background of America's horrific past. On an almost daily basis, we hear of the imminent possibility of a Second Civil War and of domestic terrorists doing everything they can to foment it. While I am certain that much of this is a scare tactic and part of the psychological war, I also recognize with Shakespeare that what's past is prologue.

The history of the United States is replete with examples of armed aggression by whites against African Americans for nothing more than being Black or being black and successful. The intent has always been to keep African Americans in their place. The tactic has always been what we now call *terrorism.*

*Terrorism is the unlawful use of violence and intimidation, especially against civilians, in the pursuit of political aims - in pursuit of political aims.* In the South terrorism was always the primary tactic. Lynching, draggings, church bombings, tar and featherings were all terrorist tools of intimidation.

The first terrorists were domestic. They called themselves the Ku Klux Klan. Many of them were judges, bankers, police and military officers. They called it the "Invisible Empire" which is an appropriate title because you never knew who belonged. That's why they wore hoods - perhaps the most cowardly of their many cowardly deeds and devices.

So when I talk about a second civil war I'm not talking about *North vs South*. I'm talking about large-scale terrorism aimed at Black communities not only but especially in the South where 56% [12]of us now reside - basically but not surprisingly - in the former Confederate states.

The terrorist's tools were designed and intended to put fear in the hearts of those who witnessed or heard of such atrocities. Interestingly, President Biden just signed the Emmet Till Anti-Lynching Act. It comes 122 years after the first bill was introduced in 1900. We may logically ask why now? Do they know something we don't know?

The point here is not that increased terrorism leading to a second civil war will happen but that given the past how can we logically dismiss the possibility that it will? Or that we might be the target? This is the reality of our past. *Past is prologue. Forewarned is forearmed*. Now for a detailed analysis of our present state.

When you see gray clouds on the horizon you know without checking with a meteorologist that a storm is coming. Smart people take preventive measures to lessen the storm's impact. Of course, there are always those who will say the storm may not develop or if it does it may not be catastrophic. But only fools ignore the signs altogether. The signs and portents today are as obvious as gray clouds.

- *Our neighborhoods are being gentrified.* We can no longer afford to live in the communities that we grew up in.

- Many of our neighborhoods have become food deserts where we pay premium prices for provisions that they would not dare to attempt to sell in upscale communities.
- Banks will not loan us money to refurbish homes but will loan to others to buy our properties at bargain prices.
- Local governments aided by the federal government are taking possession of entire communities using eminent domain and "urban blight"[13] to turn our communities over to private developers.
- Our schools are underfunded because in many states schools are funded, at least in part, by property taxes.[14] This ingenious plan enables even wealthy states to have majority underfunded schools and minority affluent schools just across the railroad tracks.
- Nearly half (44.6%) of public education funding comes from local sources most from property taxes. *These funds are raised and spent locally.*
- Fifty percent of the public school population in the United States are low-income students.
- 40% of public school students qualify for free or reduced-price lunches in 40 states. In 18 of those states, student poverty rates are over 50%.[15]
- The rise of violent White Supremacist activities throughout the United States.

We can see from the above that circumstances for African Americans are not as great as some would have us believe.

And that many Black people are suffering at a vastly dispro-
portionate rate to that of whites.

## The Enemy's Most Likely Course of Action

Following the Tactical Planning Student Handbook used
by the United States Marine Corps in its Basic Officer Course
we next look at the enemy's most likely course of action. This
part of the analysis is especially important because it requires
us to be proactive rather than reactionary.

What then will be the enemy's most likely course of action?
Again, the past is a prologue. Based on past experience we can
predict the probability of the continuation of the policies of
the recent *past with increased emphasis on reversing advances
that have been made and which if not controlled will serve
to undermine white supremacy.* Remember that after slavery
the white supremacist plan has always been to continue the
formerly enslaved in slavery in all but name.

"And what is it that we want to do? Why it is within the
limits imposed by the Federal Constitution, to establish white
supremacy in this State."[16]

This quote is from *Hunter v. Underwood,[17] a United
States Supreme Court* case in which the Court overturned an
Alabama statute that disenfranchised Blacks and whites. The
reason it was overturned was that the Alabama legislature,
in convention, explicitly stated that they wanted to establish
white supremacy. That is, they wanted to disenfranchise Black
folk wherever, whenever and however possible. Note the
subtlety of this statement; it provides another unmistakable

definition of white supremacy - *the disenfranchisement of Blacks*.

Merriam Webster's Dictionary defines franchise as "freedom from servitude or restraint[,]" and "[a]lthough *disenfranchise* does broadly signify depriving someone of any of a number of legal rights, it is most often used today of withholding the right to vote, or of the *diminished social or political status of a marginalized group.*"[18] Clearly to be disenfranchised encompassed a great deal more than voting. The connection between politics and power could not be more evident.

I cite this case because it clearly demonstrates something that we seem to have overlooked: legislators (politicians all), whether local, state or federal, can pass any law they want and the law has *presumed constitutionality until challenged and overturned*. And because the wheels of justice turn exceedingly slowly generations can go by before a wrong is righted, if at all.

The Alabama Legislators were well aware of the constraints placed upon them by the Federal Constitution and drafted their laws accordingly. Remember *Hunter* was decided in 1985. By the time the law was overturned, it had been in place for *84 years*. Five generations were disenfranchised before the law was struck down.

More importantly, *Hunter* instructed legislators on how to do it right the next time. They knew that in light of the 14th Amendment to the Constitution, they had to make the law race-neutral on its face. What they did not realize was that they had to keep their mouths shut. They couldn't make public statements about their racial animus. *Make the law race-neutral on its face then require plaintiffs to prove intent - and keep your mouth shut, is the rule established by Hunter.* Curiously, the decision was written by Chief Justice William H. Rehnquist. Need I say more?

Therefore, the enemy's course of action as always is *generational*. It is to maintain control by ensuring that each generation maintains and advances its power while ensuring that others particularly Black people the descendants of the enslaved, do not advance beyond second-class citizenship. *This involves the control of political and economic power.*

The strategy is simpler than it may seem. It is because of slavery, that is the uncompensated labor of kidnapped Africans, that they (primarily wealthy white males) were able to build without the cost of labor. Add to that the fact that the land that they were building on was taken from the Native Americans and you have a strategy that permitted them to accumulate untold *generational wealth*. In short, each generation started with an undeserved leg up that had nothing to do with merit and everything to do with robbery, kidnapping, and forced labor.

In order to maintain that undeserved economic advantage laws, policies, customs and traditions were designed, codified, and implemented to prevent each generation without wealth to continue without appreciable change in their economic circumstances from generation to generation. This is why it is said that it will take African Americans at least 228 years to attain economic parity with whites - 228 years!. "**If** current economic trends continue, the average Black household will need 228 years to accumulate as much wealth as their White counterparts hold today. Absent significant policy interventions, or a seismic change in the American economy, people of color will never close the gap."[19]

Note the author states it will take 228 years *but may never happen without policy interventions. When you hear policy think politics.* Politics is the science of power. Political parties run the government according to policies. Policies are the principles and plan of action by which the government exercises your power in the name of *"We The People"* and in accordance with the subterfuge known as the Rule of Law. After the Civil War white supremacy demanded that the formerly enslaved could not be allowed to offer their skills and their labor in private enterprise on the free market. After all, the former enslavers were now destitute and desperately needed the skills and labor of the formerly enslaved to maintain themselves and to rebuild. So laws were drafted that prohibited the formerly enslaved from hiring themselves out or owning businesses or land without the approval of good white folk.

Good white folk invented vagrancy laws, inmate leasing, chain gangs, private prisons, and mass incarceration. The strategy was to keep us, particularly Black men, as close to slavery as possible *within the limits imposed by the Federal Constitution. In order to do so, they had to codify the tactics used before the civil war in a facially race-neutral way. The purpose and intent of this tactic was and remains to destabilize the African American family unit.*

## *Destabilization of The African American Family Unit*

The family is the foundation of all civilization. Disrupt the family and you destroy the people's ability to rise above their circumstances and to prosper. It is clear that a major part and primary objective of the enemy's tactics is to disrupt the family unit. This was accomplished by devaluing the male so that he was seen as powerless and unable to protect the family.

We have felt powerless and unable to cope with threatening events since the days when we were abducted from our ancestral home, shackled and chained, buried in the holds of monstrous merchant slave ships, and brought to these shores, against our will, to be auctioned like cattle.

We were then dispersed to laboratories known as plantations where we remained for centuries under the watchful eye of vicious overseers, whips, and guns at the ready, who inflicted mortal wounds for the slightest infraction of the barbarous slave codes. We survived in abject poverty and constant humiliation. The lingering message of that dark period was that we were powerless to change our circumstances. Think about it.

- *We were powerless to rise up against our sadistic captors;*
- *We were powerless to protect our women and children;*
- *We were powerless to keep our families intact;*
- *We were powerless to publicly speak our ancestral languages;*
- *We were powerless to maintain our ancestral culture;*

- *We were powerless to invoke the Gods of our ancestors aloud;*
- *We were powerless to fight and powerless to run;*
- *We were powerless to hold property and powerless to make plans or exercise our intellects.*

*And, after so-called emancipation, we remained powerless.*

- *We were powerless to do anything that we could not do when we were legally slaves;*
- *We were powerless to travel;*
- *We were powerless to participate in the so-called democratic process;*
- *We were powerless to prevent the Ku Klux Klan from terrorizing our communities;*
- *We were powerless against the infamous Black Codes and Jumpin' Jim Crow;*
- *We were powerless to force the United States Government to come to our aid.*

Today we remain all but powerless:

- *We are powerless to prevent the mass incarceration of our men, women and children;*
- *We are still powerless to prevent the raging, virulent hostility of the judicial and legislative branches of the government toward any policy, program or philosophy that would do anything to level the playing field;*
- *We are still powerless to travel the highways and byways*

*of this land without being profiled at every stop sign and intersection;*

- *We are still powerless to prevent our communities from being redlined and designated crime and drug-infested areas;*
- *We are still powerless to stop the agents of law enforcement from ignoring the Constitution to enter our homes, businesses, houses of worship and schools without legal cause or justification and without warrants;*
- *And, we remain powerless to appoint judges who will not countenance such abuse and powerless to remove those who do.*

It follows that the most effective way to disrupt the family is also the most effective way to control the present and future generations as long as the dysfunctionality created in one generation is transmitted to the next.

We may anticipate the continuation of such policies in the near future coupled with ever increasingly more Draconian laws and the repeal of laws that have been in place since the days of the civil rights movement. Do not be surprised if cherished laws of long standing are found unconstitutional in the area of civil rights and criminal law. .

### *Caveat:*

It should be noted here that the tactics outlined here are used not only against African American descendants of the enslaved but all poor people to a greater or lesser extent. We welcome allies but we reserve the right and responsibility to always lead the charge and defend ourselves.

## *Digression: The Myth of the Rule of Law (and Other Nonsense)*

We are repeatedly reminded that America is governed by the Rule of Law and not the Rule of Men. A quaint and misleading turn of phrase. *Laws are made by men.* What they really mean is that laws, once codified, are somehow no longer the laws of men. The thing to remember is these codified laws are arbitrary because created by men *arbitrarily*. So that the result can only be the codification of arbitrary laws.

Once these are codified they are then interpreted and enforced by police, prosecutors, and judges. In the case of police, so-called peace officers, it is enforcement on the fly with the knowledge that there is little chance of them being held responsible for any of their actions. For prosecutors, it is the *unreviewable discretion* to prosecute or not and what to prosecute for. For judges, it is the *discretion* to do pretty much what they want to so long as they are acting in their official capacity as judges. In this regard It has been said that:

*"The discretion of a judge is said to be the law of tyrants. It is always unknown. It is different in different men. It is and depends upon constitution, temper and passion. In the best, it is sometimes caprice. In the worst, it is every vice, folly and passion to which human nature is liable." Justice Charles Pratt (aka Lord Camden).* [20]

Put another way, *discretion is the bane of the law*. Discretion is the power of officials to act according to the dictates of their own judgment and conscience. It should also be remembered that the poor and powerless never create laws. Put another way, every law ever passed was the creation of a politician(s) whose job it was to maintain or advance the control and authority of those in power - essentially wealthy white men. Remember *every law creates an outlaw*. Anatole France perhaps said it best:

**"The law, in its majestic equality, forbids the rich as well as the poor to sleep under bridges, to beg in the streets, and to steal bread."** Anatole France

Over the East Entrance to the United States Supreme Court, there is a sculpture of three ancient figures. Moses is at the center holding two tablets containing the Ten Commandments, on his left stands Confucius, and on his right Solon. Under it is carved the phrase "Equality under the law." The Tenth Commandment condones slavery.[21] So much for the Rule of Law.

### The United States is a Democracy

Presidents frequently refer to "our democracy" and state unabashedly that "the United States is a democracy" or that the founders created a democracy. In a recent speech, President Biden referred to the United States as a democracy thirty-one times. In his Independence Hall speech in September

2023, President Biden said, "For a long time, we've reassured ourselves that American democracy is guaranteed," "But it is not. We have to defend it. Protect it. Stand up for it. Each and every one of us."

We also hear inaccurate talk about how this or that person or group is trying to undermine our cherished democracy. From scholars and historians (who certainly should know better) to respected news networks and Pulitzer prize-winning reporters we hear the same patently inaccurate line - America is a democracy. Nothing could be further from the truth. Now some people may argue that this is nitpicking, I beg to differ. Suppose you ordered a vacuum cleaner and they sent you a broom. Would you just accept it? Of course not. So the question becomes why would anyone repeatedly refer to a broom as a vacuum cleaner? And try to sell you one for the other?

So for the record, the United States is not now nor has it ever been a democracy. The word democracy is not even mentioned in the United States Constitution. However, the Constitution clearly and unequivocally states: "The United States shall guarantee to every state in this union a Republican Form of Government." *United States Constitution, Article IV.*


*The Exploitation Plan:*
*Attack The Enemy's Center of Gravity*


The Marine Tactical Planning Handbook requires us to next develop an *exploitation plan*. The exploitation plan requires us to discover the enemy's center of gravity and devise a plan to attack it. The enemy's center of gravity is his critical vulnerability. The exploitation plan must be designed to find and strike at this vulnerability.

*Locating the Enemy's Center of Gravity*
*The enemy's center of gravity is that element or capability which allows the enemy to execute his mission or scheme of maneuver successfully.* In most cases, the enemy will have multiple centers of gravity. In our case, the enemy does, in fact, have multiple centers of gravity. For our purposes, these are *politics/law and the economy.* These are the areas that allow the enemy to maneuver successfully. And the place where the enemy's greatest vulnerabilities are to be found.

## Politics and Law

I identified politics and law first and together because they support each other and in fact, have a symbiotic relationship. Politicians create the law and are very often lawyers. Judges who interpret the law are often lawyers. In some states, you must have a law degree to become a judge. Politics cannot be divorced from the law. Their relationship is indeed symbiotic in that each depends on the other for survival or in this case for power.

**"Historically, lawyers have not only monopolized positions in the court system but have also dominated the political leadership of the United States. Since indepen-**

dence, more than half of all presidents, vice presidents, and members of Congress have come from a law background."[22]

### *The Economy*

The economy is a center of gravity because of the enemy's need to produce goods and services for domestic and foreign consumption. This does not imply or mean disruption of the economy but rather strategically targeted use of the power of the dollar.

For example, a business that is physically in a Black community owes a great deal to its patrons because its only customers come from the surrounding community. Likewise, businesses that are not physically in the community are dependent on our dollars in direct proportion to the percentage of their sales our patronage represents.

I intentionally use the word *patron* rather than consumer because a patron is a person who gives financial support to a person or organization. Every dollar that we spend with these businesses represents financial support. Some people may argue that these businesses are doing us a favor by opening shops in our communities. This is a mentality that serves only to justify our supporting businesses that benefit other communities.

## CHAPTER FOUR

# Power

I have been warned not to use the word power because of its negative connotation and the fact that many people, African Americans, and others, are *afraid* of the term. It seems that there is a school of thought in the African American community that effectively exercises self-censorship by refusing to discuss and now even mention words or concepts that are not approved for our use by white folks and their sycophants.

A perfect example is the age-old warning that we Black folk must never discuss religion or politics. Really? Why not? The same people can be heard at every turn proclaiming that freedom of speech is not only a constitutional right but also the very essence of our liberty. In fact, some argue that freedom of expression is the essence of democracy. Whether that is true or not, freedom of speech is the right to express any opinions without censorship or restraint.

The point here is that it is patently ridiculous to argue that I should not use a word because people, white or Black, are afraid of it. More importantly, it is indicative of the effectiveness of the centuries of indoctrination intended to prevent the enslaved from ever thinking in terms of freedom in any form. I refuse to fall into that trap. So if you are truly among the group of people who are afraid of or in some way discomforted by the mere mention of the word power, this book is not for you. Final question: why would we stop using terms simply because they scare white folks or alert them to our quest for power? *I'll wait.*

## *What is Power?*

Power, * is a word that is used repeatedly by people who have little first-hand knowledge of it. We speak of power with a familiarity that seems to indicate an intimate, pre-existing relationship with it. Yet, our inability to effect meaningful change in our life circumstances and those of the people to whom we owe the duty of protection and care belies the existence of such a relationship.

Power is such that even in the absence of an intimate relationship with it we instinctively respond to its presence. When someone with power speaks, we are immediately attentive. The mere vocalization of the word raises our expectations and manifests the sensory experience of what it must actually be like to possess it. Not to mention that those who have power are the first to deny that they have it and to argue that power corrupts. Whether it does or not there is not a single example in history of a person who voluntarily gave up his power or taught others how to get it.

"Power is not an institution and not a structure; neither is it a certain strength we are endowed with; it is the name that one attributes to a complex strategical situation in a particular society." Michel Foucault[23]


## *So, what is power?*

*Power is both a physical substance and an idea.* It is energy and thought, process and principle, reality and potential. As physical substance power is defined by the law of physics. Physics is the science of the properties of matter and energy. It defines power as a physical substance because power is both energy and matter. It can be defined, therefore, by the law of quantum, atomic and nuclear physics as well. Power as an idea, is best understood as the science of politics. We will cover this aspect of power in depth in the chapter on politics.

*Power is neutral and expansive.* Because of its neutrality, it will serve any master. Because of its inherently expansive nature, it will reward the master whom it serves with ever-increasing portions of it and will do so without remorse or compassion. In order to acquire and utilize power, its elements both substantial and theoretical, must be identified and understood.

*Power in the mathematical sense.* In the mathematical sense power is the result obtained when a quantity is multiplied by itself a specified number of times. The product of self-multiplication is always exponential. As a result, power can also be accurately defined as an exponential increase in a base quantity that is determined by the number of times the quantity is multiplied by itself.

Power may be broadly characterized as *force, energy,* and *strength* depending on the way it functions at any given time. Power/energy are the keys to all activity on Earth. Force and strength are applied and stored power respectively. Force is simply any kind of push or pull. It is the *application* of power. Potential energy is energy that is stored, and available for use. Strength is simply the innate capacity of a thing to resist or endure. It is the power of opposition.

Power is, therefore, a composite of force, energy and strength. It is force when it is exerted; energy when it is creative or in motion; strength when it causes things to resist or endure.

Recap: *Power is both a physical substance and an idea that is both neutral and expansive. It serves any master without remorse or compassion and when held will increase at an exponential and predictable rate.*


### The Power Principle

*Power is also a principle.* It is a fundamental, universal law from which many others derive. Simply stated the Power Principle provides that *those who have power shall prosper, and those who do not shall serve.* Given the implications of the Power Principle, it is inescapable that knowledge of the substance of power is insufficient to assure that we acquire and utilize power proportionate to our numbers. We must also analyze the idea and theory of power.

The Power Principle is best observed through the science of politics, which is, more concisely, the science of the acquisition, utilization, distribution, and control of power in the governance of human affairs.

It is in the political arena that power is most profitably observed. In politics, we can see, through the long lens of history, the importance of power to the development and maintenance of cultural identity. For it is the relative amount of power held by one country vis-a-vis others that determines its relative position in the world of nations.

Intranationally, that is within a nation, the power dynamics are the same. *Groups within a given nation will be influential and prosperous according to the amount of power they control relative to other groups within that nation.* Indeed, every aspect of governance from law and morality to poverty and affluence is informed by the wishes and worldview of the dominant culture. The dominant culture is such, of course, precisely because of its control of power and the power-driven technology known as government.

### The Power Process

Power is also an observable process. When it flows it is like an electrical current, either direct or alternating. When its flow is regular it appears as a structure. When it moves quickly and takes an irregular course it is more characteristic of what is generally understood as a process.

Power's ability to alternate is an apparently fixed reality. Like electricity, power may be static, appearing randomly causing dormant power to be released wherever friction occurs. This may explain the collective feeling of power experienced by rioters whose random action, like static electricity, causes the release of power, albeit destructively. The flow or current of power may also be generated purposefully and from a specific location.

Power, like electricity, always exists somewhere. The power process is contributed to by all people. Most are unaware of their contribution and are, therefore, more or less *inactive participants* in its use. Others, always a minority, are more or less active and in control of greater power not because they are inherently more powerful, but because they have gained control of the power of the inactive participants.

The inactive participants are actually the majority because they contribute the bulk of the power. It is an unalterable and universal law that power always resides with the inactive majority and can never reside elsewhere. *It is also they who unwittingly dictate the course of action a leader will take.*

If the leader discerns that the group will accept crumbs in lieu of real positive accomplishments, he will lead them to the crumbs that will mark his success. If, however, the group seeks the entire loaf, the leader's success is measured by that standard. In short, they dictate what course the leader will take by what they will accept. Perhaps Frederick Douglass said it best, "The limits of tyrants are prescribed by the endurance of those whom they oppress."

In short, we have the power, presently dormant, to direct the course of future events to ensure we are no longer taken for granted and that we receive our fair share of the wealth of this nation proportional to our numbers in the population.

## *The Law of Power Units*

As individuals each of us is a self-contained power not unlike a cellular battery. When batteries are used to power a device a small device may require only one battery while a larger device may require multiple batteries. One AAA battery will power a penlight while as many as 12 D batteries may be needed to power a large flashlight. The power must be suited to the job. And needless to say, a device that requires 12 batteries will not operate with only 11.

When individuals have a common goal and objective, join together we multiply ourselves and our combined power will exceed the total of our individual power by a measurable, predictable, and exponential rate of increase. In short, the whole is greater than the sum of its parts.

A power unit is composed of an individual and his/her *power set.* A power set is the individual power unit plus the skills and resources he/she brings to the table. Skills are broadly defined as expertise in a given field. This could include anything from carpentry to construction to customer service to management to entrepreneurship. Resources are broadly defined as contacts (friends, relatives, associates, coworkers), finances, and influence. It follows that each of us is a self-contained power unit but each of us is potentially a power set.

Although it is true that we cannot, at least mathematically, multiply ourselves. One times one will always be one. One to the first power is always one. But as soon as we join with other power units, multiplication is possible. Two power units are the energetic or power equivalent of two to the second power (2x2 = 4); three power units combined represent (3x3x3 =27) twenty-seven units of power. If the quantity is energy/power then the formula where AP= pn is Active Power, p is a power unit, and n is the number of times the power unit is multiplied by itself, is suggested.

Put another way, when "power units" are multiplied by themselves the actual increase in their combined energy level is always exponential. In order to fully understand power both active and dormant, we must also examine power in regard to the different ways it may be manifested. We will address the powerful implications of this in the section on Critical Mass (CM). For now, just understand that we are approximately 48 million strong and have a gross domestic product of approximately $1.2 trillion, and 47% of us own our homes. We frequently use this power to finance the building of our churches. What if we used it for something more profitable than building churches?

## CHAPTER FIVE

# Politics

## *Introduction*

It has always been curious if not baffling to me why coming up we were always cautioned never to discuss religion or politics. As I grew older, I began to question and then challenge the idea because it made no sense to me. How could we confront the system that oppresses us without talking about it? That was until I realized the purpose of such a counter-productive idea. If politics can be said to control us but we do not discuss it we will never be able to develop effective strategies to confront it. In short, we can never obtain true freedom until we master politics - to master a thing we must know exactly what it is.

## *What is Politics?*

The word politics comes from the ancient Greek word *polis* meaning city-state. But as to the modern definition of politics, there seems to be no real agreement. I submit this is wholly intentional.

The most frequently advanced definition is that politics is the science of government. This definition is far too restrictive and is frankly misleading because politics is not as much about government as it is about who controls the government and how control is acquired and maintained. For the record, I am not alone in this view. One observer points out that "[p]olitics is the science of who gets what, when, and how . . . . [m]odern political theories conform to this definition as it establishes the unique connection of politics and power.

Power creates structures and explains the struggle among individuals or groups of individuals. It is in this sense that politics deviates from ethics inasmuch as *any means* could be used to get whatever is desired and whenever it is desired for as long as it serves the purpose."[24]

Although it is true that politics can be usefully defined as the science of government, it is equally true that a particular government, the policies it enacts, the laws it promulgates and enforces, are a direct result of the customs, world-view, traditions, and heritage, hence, the culture of the dominant political group. In this sense, it is the culture that informs the policies of the government as well as the views and perspectives of those who comprise the particular governing group.

Politics, as the term is used here, shall be defined as the science of the *acquisition, distribution, utilization, and control of power in the governance of human affairs.* The science of politics is, therefore, the science of power.

## CHAPTER SIX

# Political Power

*Introduction*

*"The greatest power is not money power,*
*but political power." Walter Annenberg*

*In its political manifestation power is the ability to take uni-*
*lateral action in the face of the existence of actual or potential*
*resistant force and to succeed in doing so.*

Political power is the triumph of the will of one people
over that of others. It is the force that overcomes resistance.
It is, at the same time, the strength of opposition and the
audacity of confrontation.

Political power is manifested in the acceptance by others
of your right to take action, that is, to use power in ways that
you deem legitimate. Authority cannot exist without power
because authority is *defined as the "legitimate" power of a*
*person or group over other people. This power becomes legitimate*
*because it is codified, that is, written into law. And by that*

*process creates the right to give orders and enforce obedience. Of course, the laws are never written by poor people, more precisely never written by people who have not realized the power they possess. Politicians write the laws and they have the power to do that because we wittingly or unwittingly gave it to them.*

Power becomes institutionalized or accepted by cloaking it in the guise of authority. In order to have maximum effectiveness political power must be codified in laws and regulations that are themselves based upon the traditions and norms, that is the culture, of the group that comprises the society.

Here we have the marriage of politics and culture that I refer to as political culture that gives rise to political organization. Political organization is a relationship. It is that which exists when power units combine for a stated purpose. It is the order of collective human affairs. Since the order is imposed it is a regulation consisting of rules promulgated by those whose superior power permits them to make the rules in the first place.

Digression: Political Culture

A brief digression is necessary here on the concept of political culture. Political culture is the marriage of politics and culture. It is a separate branch of culture that deals exclusively with the acquisition of power. Like all cultures, it represents the worldview of a particular people, developed over time, and reverently handed down to succeeding generations. It represents the tactics and techniques, acquisition and control of power in sufficient amounts to insure the survival and prosperity of a particular group of people. It is the *corpus* of knowledge, information, and concepts of the group regarding the nature, properties, and elements of power.

*Political culture is historical and ancestral.* In the state of nature, it was confined to clan activities. As populations grew and sedentary existence flourished it was extended to new inter-tribal and national activities that required pre-set rules to ensure order and efficiency. For this reason, political culture became a form of initiation. The political initiation process would have had at least three characteristics.

- First, it requires initiation into a general culture which would have been accomplished at the family level or in age groups.
- Second, there would have been an initiation into political culture, at least for those who would someday rule, which would amount to an education in the science of politics.
- Finally, there would have been the recruitment and training of persons for specific functions in the political system and the deployment of those so trained.

In the most effective application of these principles, the initiation into political culture would have occurred simultaneously with the initiation into the general culture. Political culture is important to the understanding of political power because there is a vital connection between general and political culture. It is the worldview of the dominant general culture, its values, and beliefs, that the political culture strengthens and supports. To this end, the education system always functions to maintain the cultural and political status quo.

When a political culture governs people of diverse cultural backgrounds it tends to develop an undercurrent of agitation that remains always just below the deceptively calm surface. This stems from the fact that while most people tend to view politicians cynically, they also believe that the political process works in the end.

The agitation arises from the fact that within the society there is always another group whose tendency is to develop a radical view and who believe that political change can only come as a result of violent upheaval. The agitation is similar to that produced by the tectonic plates of the Earth's crust. The plates rub against each other, below the surface, almost imperceptibly, until they cause an earthquake. The process is slow, but the result is inevitable.

*The United States of America is a political culture.* African Americans are by and large, descendants of enslaved Africans who have been left stranded by time and technology. To the American political culture, African Americans having built this country with their forced, uncompensated labor are now much like the appendix - we have outlived our usefulness.

We have learned to imitate America's general culture well. We have not, however, mastered its political culture. African Americans have come to believe, like many White Americans, that the political system can be reformed and that the lofty pronouncements upon which it is based actually govern the distribution of power and privilege. This is perhaps understandable of white Americans who have seen their fortunes increase over the years and who have always had the reassurance that the people who were running things were, at least, of their "race".

In the case of African Americans, the belief is absurd despite the large numbers of us who profess to believe it. Logic would seem to dictate that African Americans, perhaps more than any other group of Americans, would be overwhelmingly in the ranks of those who hold the radical view and who believe that political change in America can only result from violent upheaval.

This paradox arises from our lack of familiarity with the concepts of Authentic Ancestral Culture and its counterpart which may be called Authentic Political Culture. Authentic Political Culture is the way of governance, the rules of government, and the science of politics as developed by a specific group of people, over time, and handed down to succeeding generations to ensure their political survival and prosperity.

Having failed to understand the importance of political culture we have likewise misapprehended the importance of Authentic Political Culture. The result is that we have been unable to understand the dynamics of the political culture in which we find ourselves. The situation of African Americans is also distinct from that of White Americans because we are a minority that cannot become part of the national political culture that dictates the rights and privileges under which we are forced to live. Our inability to do so is a direct result of the refusal of the dominant political culture to accept us as equals. We must, therefore, begin to think in terms of not only Authentic Political Culture but also national political culture.

It should be noted here that nationalism and national

political culture are not the same. *Nationalism is self-determination. National political Culture is the method by which nationalism is achieved.* National political culture has two components. It consists of a professional political group, always relatively small, that promulgates the rules, and a significantly larger group that is expected to abide by those rules. The true distinction in the two groups is that the former is knowledgeable in the science of power while the latter is not. It is this passive arrangement that permits the development of the national political culture. Even when the larger group is literate they tend not to involve themselves in the political process being satisfied with abiding by the rules promulgated by the "professionals".

Another factor is that the larger group is always a mix of persons from different backgrounds and degrees of political sophistication and involvement. The smaller group, on the other hand, is generally composed of persons more nearly homogeneous in at least one characteristic, wealth. The effect of this is best illustrated by the bicameral system of governance employed in the United States.

In a bicameral system, a larger body and a smaller body make the laws. But why, it may be logically asked, are two legislatures required? The answer may be found in the history of the United States Congress:

The United States House of Representatives was referred to by the Framers of the Constitution as the "House of Rabble". The term is one of contempt for the masses or common people who would be represented there. The United States Senate, on the other hand, was to be the "House of the Aristocracy" the landed gentry."

The bicameral or two-house system serves one purpose. It ensures that the rich (always a minority) will have veto power over the ability of the poor (always a majority) to enact legislation that addresses their needs. Why else would a system be installed that requires that bills be passed in identical form by both houses before they may be forwarded to the president to become law? Of course, the notion that the rich will ever agree to provide meaningful assistance to the poor sufficient to lift them from their poverty is utopian at best and preposterous at worst. The old saying that "poverty is the rich man's cow" is particularly appropriate here.

Moreover, it is this same mix that determines such fundamental matters as what makes government lawful; what power may leaders and their delegates lawfully exercise; how citizens may or may not organize in opposition to their leaders; and how power is transferred. In each of these categories, those who rule (politicians are literally rulers) have a vested interest in ensuring that the lawful government is favorable to their present and future interests; that leaders shall have virtually unlimited power that is, in appearance, limited; and that the transfer shall be carefully controlled.

In a political culture where the political initiation process is separate from the general cultural initiation, a class of professionals known as politicians arise. These soon become defenders of a vested interest in their privileged positions and lose sight of their sworn obligation to those who they profess to represent. This further exacerbates the inherent agitation in the political culture. Since they will forever be at odds with their constituents, the longer they hold office the greater the distance between them will become.

Political culture also serves the purpose of defining how and when power may be used within the group and within the community of nations. Because political culture is a body of ideas regarding power, it must include power messages as the core of its language.

Power messages are the words and symbols that instill the belief in one's ability to excel by virtue of the connection to a glorious past and the vision of a prosperous future. They are based on the achievement of our ancestors who fought and succeeded. Political culture too is part of the power dynamic that is the *raison d'etre* of the New Body Politic.

Political power is generated by collective action. It comes into existence when and only when the group decides to act as one. Collective goals born of collective vision become collective mandates. Because politics also involves conflict and confrontation over the control of power, those who act collectively and decisively are most successful in obtaining their goals.

Political power may be enhanced or undermined if the general culture sends mixed messages to some or all of its citizens. If the general culture is one that is founded on suspicion of all people, the people who adhere to it will see others as generally dishonest and untrustworthy. As a result, their ability to act collectively will be undermined. General culture can, therefore, undermine or destroy the development of national political culture and simultaneously prevent the acquisition of political power.

Political power is also undermined when the general culture teaches that positive change can be effected through collective action but the reality experienced by a particular group within the society is that of political impotence. In such a case the group tends to see politics as inconsequential or concludes that their failure at the science of power is in some way a result of their own actions.

By contrast, a general culture that respects and incorporates national political culture tends to produce individuals who view themselves as politically savvy, capable of political conquest, and entitled to political power at least proportionate to their numbers.

In the case of African Americans, it is apparent that we have succumbed to the belief that we are dishonest and untrustworthy and the reality that we are politically impotent. The combination has all but removed our ability to see ourselves as politically powerful people capable of taking unilateral action to change our collective circumstances for the better. Without the ability to see ourselves in this way we have effectively handed our fair share of political power over to enemies who have used it against us.

## The Political Power Base

The Political Power base is like a magnetic field and its creation is absolutely necessary if we are to reverse our unfortunate political circumstances. Each of us is an energetic, self-contained power unit. The law of power units dictates that when we combine we increase our power exponentially. When we do so we create a group field that is analogous to a magnetic field. A group field is a vital force at the center of the national consciousness created by the power of the collective will. The group field is the center of the political power base.

*The power base is not, however, the people themselves. It is the power that is generated by their relationship.* It is virtually unlimited power hidden in each individual that is only energized when the individuals combine in a purposeful, harmonious relationship. The stronger the power base the greater its ability to overcome resistance and opposition,

The power base, in turn, resides within a Body Politic. It cannot exist without it. It is for this reason that power must be made to appear centered in one person who seems to control it and who can bring it to bear on any obstacle. *It is a focused power that gains attention and is respected.* Once a power base is developed the mere use of its power both increases its numbers and multiplies its power exponentially. This is because of the fact that power is neutral and expansive and the operation of the law of power units.

## CHAPTER SEVEN

# Critical Mass

### INTRODUCTION

**"When the size of the group supporting your cause reaches a critical mass, any legislator or elected official has to pay attention." Mark Shields**

Energy and power are synonymous terms. Energy is related to mass. Under certain conditions, mass can be transformed into energy. The rate at which the transformation takes place is fixed. The fixed exchange rate of mass to energy is represented in Einstein's now famous equation $E=Mc2$. The equation implies that the exchange rate of mass to energy is a universal law. It also indicates that a small amount of mass transforms into a tremendous amount of energy or power. As we will see Critical Mass is a condition precedent to the release of energy.

Power, therefore, follows Critical Mass at a fixed and predictable rate. When Critical Mass is attained, and the necessary preconditions are in place, a chain reaction is set in motion that culminates in the explosive release of energy according to the mass-energy exchange rate embodied in Einstein's equation.

When Critical Mass is understood as the minimum number of enriched persons necessary to sustain a political/cultural chain reaction the result and its potential impact on the course of future human events is explosive and revolutionary. *The attainment of Critical Mass is, therefore, the single most important objective of any organization whose sincere goal is the empowerment of African Americans.*

It follows that the release of energy that will precipitate the radical revolutionary political/cultural chain reaction awaits the accumulation of Critical Mass. But Critical Mass is more than mere numbers. The type of people needed for Critical Mass are those who have been enriched. *Enrichment is the process of enlightenment by which people of ordinary intelligence, capability, and determination are transformed into persons of extraordinary intellect, selfless leadership potential, and transcendent will by the attainment of clarity of vision.*

The number of people required for Critical Mass is directly related to the type of people (enriched or unenriched) who will be mass. The number of enriched persons in the core Critical Mass determines its concentration. A high concentration of enriched persons has two advantageous effects: (1) smaller numbers are required to attain Critical Mass, and (2) the amount of energy or power released increases in direct proportion to the percentage of the core that is enriched. Therefore, the energy level or explosive potential of the cultural/political chain reaction is directly related to its concentration.

In our cultural/political chain reaction knowledge and information form the equivalent of neutrons in the nuclear process. Like its counterpart in nuclear physics, this knowledge is neutral. As used here neutral means accurate and unbiased. Once a sufficient number of persons are enriched, and the Critical Mass is thereby attained, the energy released may be used to either create an explosion or to generate energy to accomplish collective goals or both.

## *Critical Mass Summary*

- The concept of Critical Mass (CM) is based, by analogy, on the process of nuclear fission by which atoms are split to create the release of energy in a nuclear bomb or a nuclear reactor. Energy and power are synonymous terms.
- The attainment of CM is, in the cultural/political sense, the single most important objective of any organization whose goal is the empowerment of African Americans.
- CM is the minimum number of "enriched" persons necessary to launch a cultural/political chain reaction.
- Enrichment is the process of enlightenment by which people of ordinary intelligence, capability, and determination are transformed into persons of extraordinary intellect, selfless leadership potential, and transcendent will by the attainment of a clear vision.
- When CM is attained it will make possible the release of energy/power that will launch radical, revolutionary,

cultural/political chain reactions that will transform our thinking and our lives forever.

- The number of enriched persons required to attain CM is determined by the following equation: $CM = \varphi(AAP)$, where CM is Critical Mass, $\varphi$ (PHI) is the ratio of 1:1.618, and AAP is the African American Population.

*This formula indicates that less than two percent of our people, having been properly enriched, can create the explosive impact, radical change, and radiant growth that will be the result of the cultural/political chain reaction.*

In the case of South Carolina specifically, the number is approximately 24,000 enriched persons of the total African American population of 1,350,000.

## CHAPTER EIGHT

# Leadership

"NO ONE LIKES THE WARRIOR UNTIL THE
ENEMY IS AT THE GATE." AFRICAN PROVERB

We have attempted to outline the contours of an urgent crisis confronting African Americans. The crisis is exacerbated by instability in our political, economic, and cultural affairs. Because the crisis arises from a set of historical factors that are unlikely to change we require a well-conceived and aggressively pursued plan of action. But no matter how well-conceived the plan is, it must be implemented. Implementation requires leadership. *Leaders must be warriors.*

To that end, we will now examine the fundamentals of leadership. We must admit at the outset that we are in a time of crisis. The Chinese hold that the notion of crisis implies both danger and opportunity. In the case of African Americans, we have to realize that danger is all around us. And the real possibility exists of a second civil war or worse. The opportunity is for us to pull together at a new level of consciousness and amass the power to change our circumstances regardless of the resistance and opposition. This requires the acquisition, utilization, distribution, and control of our enormous, latent, and dormant power.

This opportunity is perhaps the last one that we will have to marshal our collective energy to launch a preemptive attack that will save us and our children from annihilation. These words may seem harsh but whether harsh or not it cannot be disputed that the signs of a frontal assault on our liberties and our lives are afoot. That this assault is not unlike that of the 1860s and the century that followed. To ignore the possibility of an outright violent, physical assault on African American people and communities in conjunction with a political, judicial assault on our hard-earned rights is not a conspiracy theory but a valid probability based on both historic and current events.

Our problem is that we are a people who have suffered from a lack of effective leadership that has prevented us from meeting the obstacles that have thwarted our every attempt to secure our rightful share of the power and resources of the world. This is not to say that we have not had an abundance of media-generated, government-endorsed, self-proclaimed leaders. Despite the proliferation of such leaders there continues to be a longstanding vacuum in leadership in the African American community. Note that the vacuum is stated as one of leadership, not leaders.

There is a fundamental difference between the related but distinct concepts of leader and leadership. This important distinction has been tragically overlooked in our unplanned and therefore unguided quest for power and self-determination.

*A leader is simply one who goes before.* The position of first in line does not require talent, intelligence, or leadership. The first horse in a team of harnessed horses is the leader but its direction, speed, and destination are determined by the crack of the driver's whip. When it is further considered that the horse is arguably the least intelligent animal on the planet the analogy is instructive.

*The leader is distinct from the leadership.* The suffix "ship" means to create. When it is appended to the word leader it transforms it into a quality. Quality is the essential nature of a thing. Leadership is, therefore, a *creative force* that is the quality of the one who goes before. Leaders articulate, implement, and facilitate the creative force. But, leadership *creates*. That which creates must precede that which is created. Our failure to understand this distinction accounts, in large measure, for our inability to acquire the power necessary to change our circumstances for the better. Let us look at the concept of leadership to see where and how we have gone wrong.

## The Ancient Origins of Leadership

The ancient origins of leadership are to be found in the first group of humans who gathered around a favorite watering hole, and were illuminated by the understanding of two fundamental principles of survival: (1) that there is safety in numbers; and (2) that when one individual in the group sounds the danger alarm it is better to flee immediately rather than to search for the source of the danger.

Thus, it was the threat of predation that gave rise to social groups and, in turn, the reliance upon one person whose visual and hearing acuity provided a reliable, early warning system that maximized the group's ability to survive. Eventually, the experience and dominance of the savviest individual led to his or her acknowledgment by all as the leader, that is the person to whom all others looked to warn and direct in times of danger.

These principles dictated, over time, that individuals did not leave the group to venture out alone which policy, in turn, gave rise to group cohesiveness. The whole group moved from one place to another or no one did, giving rise to unity of action and simultaneity of movement. This fledgling social structure required an effective communication system between the persons who formed the group. The system of sounds, probably initiated by the same person who warned and directed in times of danger, became the forerunner of all languages. In time these social groups organized patterns that represented divisions in responsibility such as food gathering, hunting, defense, child rearing, war, and survival planning. The concept of leadership was, therefore, a necessary component of the development of group survival.

It follows that in its formative stages leadership consisted of an effective early warning system. This survival mechanism was also a defensive mechanism that was based on vision, hearing, and the ability to communicate information in an immediately understandable language and in a timely manner.

The components of the early warning system were developed from the techniques used by the one who marched at the head of the group as they traveled through perilous surroundings in their daily search for food. *The leaders came and went. It was the components, mechanisms, and techniques of leadership that were the progenitors and guardians of group survival, evolution, and ultimately civilization. Group survival and prosperity are, therefore, leadership oriented.*

Leadership is the quality a person must have to be an effective leader. Among these qualities would have been the ability to guide or show the way by going in advance, by walking at the head of the group. Therefore, the leader guides by way of example, by becoming a model.

In the absence of language, she could only teach by doing. Since the leader was always in front, she was not only the early warning system incarnate, but she was also the first to see the enemy and the first to engage him in battle. When the leader said fight, they fought. When the leader said retreat, they fled with the swiftness of the gazelle.

Unfortunately, not all leaders exhibit the qualities of leadership. In today's world, the so-called leader shows up after the event, after the danger is over, and imposes him/herself at the head and becomes the self-appointed spokesman by commandeering the microphone, and we allow them to do so.

To identify the qualities of leadership we must isolate the individual elements or ingredients of which it is composed. We must also determine the attributes of leadership that cause people to follow. We note here that the relationship between leadership and followership is symbiotic and codependent. We should also note here that leadership is a *group dynamic* because in its highest and purest expression, it is manifested by a group of people acting together.

*The first quality of leadership is the willingness to be at the front of the line.* It is a defining quality because it necessarily implies the potential of dying first in battle. The one who walks in front is the first target of the enemy. This may seem a minor requirement but it is not. It affords a process of elimination. The coward, the squeamish, the faint of heart will never elect to be at the head of the line. Persons of that ilk eliminate themselves.

*The leader's function then, is to facilitate the process of leadership.* She guides and articulates. That which she guides, that which she articulates, is *the plan of action that must always precede the leader.*

Leaders must have the ability to think for themselves, but they must do so within the parameters established, in advance, by the plan of action. When the plan of action reaches its limit, it must necessarily advance to the next level because the plan of action is always growing and evolving. It must set new parameters in order to avoid stagnation and death. As a result, the plan of action cannot be static. Leadership cannot be static either. When a thing arrives at its limit and advances to the next level of development it is being creative, innovative, and reproductive. *Leadership is also, therefore, the process that facilitates growth.*

*Leadership is a Group Dynamic* because it is a quality whose elements can be known and can also be taught. If it can be taught to anyone it can be taught to all. When leadership is taught to all of the members of the group the result is a group of persons who are willing and able to walk in front whenever the need arises. This creates a *leadership reserve.* The implications of these simple observations are staggering.

A group that maintains a leadership reserve cannot be

defeated for the reason that they will never be without carefully selected and rigorously trained leaders who can and will assume the mantle of leadership at a moment's notice. *We must cultivate leadership - not leaders.*

# CHAPTER NINE

# The New Body Politic

A body politic is a group of people organized politically and culturally in a system and structure that so mirrors that of the human body, in its key functions and composition, as to be identical to a living organism.

The form of a body politic is a political organization. Because it is composed of human beings it is a living organism as well. Like any living organism, it must be born. All living things are born of seed. *The seed of the political organization is an idea.*

It is, therefore, a seed/idea that must precede the birth of each new body politic. A seed/idea whose time has finally come will take root and a political organization will grow from it and will prosper. If the seed/idea is untimely or ill-conceived the political organization will be stillborn or hopelessly deformed and ineffective for the purpose for which it was conceived. Political organisms like all living things have a life cycle - they age and inevitably die.

A timely, well-conceived seed/idea consists of formal, detailed procedures for the recruitment, training, and coordination of the political and cultural activities of a group of people specifically formulated for the purpose of carrying out their collective and predetermined will.

Like the human body, the body politic is also composed of individual cells. Cells are literally the building blocks of life. The vital characteristic of the cell is its ability to grow. Growth in cells is a process of division or fission. Cells grow individually and when they reach the limit of their growth they divide. This innate propensity to divide is the reproductive system of the cell. All cells of the human body reproduce by the process of division. Growth is marked, therefore, by the increase in the number of cells. That which is not actively growing is actively dying. Each cell contains a power-generating plant which it creates the energy by which it sustains its life. When cells are combined it is their cumulative energy that powers the entire organism through a network of energy transmitters.

Each cell is an energy source with its own surrounding energy field. When energy fields combine the energy of the whole organism is increased exponentially creating, thereby, a group field. It is this combined energy that serves as the strength and energetic force of the body politic.

It is this hidden, unfocused, and diffuse power that leadership successfully channels for the benefit of the Body Politic and which the unscrupulous, self-anointed leader uses for his/her benefit alone. A leader who has not been carefully selected and trained to implement and articulate the plan that has preceded her will always tend toward conspicuous consumption and the abuse of power.

This is because she never learned that power is generated at high voltage and transmitted at an even higher voltage. But electricity at high voltage does not light the bulb, it burns it out. At high voltage power will electrocute rather than illuminate. The leader is the conductor of the power, not the power itself. He or she is the person who assists in the acquisition and transmission of the power for the benefit of the true owner - the Body Politic. This is why leadership is so vitally important in our continuing quest for political power proportionality.

Critical Mass is vital to the establishment of the collective, living human organism that I refer to as the New Body Politic. The New Body Politic is, for all intents and purposes, a living organism. Like any living organism, the body politic must be born. Birth requires ovum and sperm. In the New Body Politic, the ovum is represented by the existing population of African Americans. The sperm is represented by those enriched persons, male and female who comprise the Critical Mass (CM).

Those persons who comprise the enriched Critical Mass carry within them the seed/idea that will inseminate or fertilize the population and begin the rapid growth of the New Body Politic. Just as in the case of a living organism when fertilization takes place the sperm fuses with the nucleus of the ovum and an entirely new nucleus is formed. Thereafter, the process of cell division or fission begins, and birth takes place, predictably, 280 days later.

Suffice it to say that when Critical Mass is viewed as the sperm that impregnates the existing population of African

Americans with its powerful seed/idea another form of fission associated with Critical Mass is demonstrated.

As we noted in the chapter on Critical Mass less than two percent of our people having been properly enriched can generate the explosive impact, radical change, and radiant growth that will result in the necessary and long-awaited cultural/ political chain reaction.

## CHAPTER TEN

# Strategic Economics

*Economics is here defined as the use of strategic planning and tactics to achieve economic leverage and thereby community empowermenStrategict.* By the use of strategic economics, it is our intention to compel economic entities to change their policies or behavior with regard to the African American community.

*Strategic Economics is a form of economic warfare.* Economic warfare is the use of, or the threat to use, economic means against a country in order to weaken its economy and thereby reduce its political and military power. Economic warfare also includes the use of economic means to compel an adversary to change its policies or behavior or to undermine its ability to conduct normal relations with other countries.

Although we are not a country, our GDP makes us the 15th-largest economy in the world. It is time that we began to act like it.

Let us define our terms. "Strategy is the science and art of employing the political, economic, psychological, and military forces of a nation or group of nations to afford the maximum support to adopted policies in peace or war." Economics is the branch of knowledge concerned with the production, consumption, and transfer of wealth."

Strategic Economics, then, is the employment of knowledge about the production, consumption, and transfer of wealth to support our objective to attain power proportionality in all areas including but not limited to economics, by the targeted use of our $1.2 trillion dollar GDP.

Strategic economics looks at the products and services that we support to determine to what extent the financial success of these products and services is dependent on our support. We then look at how these companies are or are not supportive of our community and national interests by their willingness to support the community in return. This is, therefore, both a community and national strategy. A few examples will suffice:

- Certain ethnic groups come into our community and open businesses but do not hire our people and often treat us disrespectfully. These businesses provide niche services that we could easily do without if we understood that each dollar spent with these businesses represents support for businesses that will not hire our people.
- There are also those who routinely spend money to reach our communities but do not spend money with African American businesses while paying outsiders to reach us.

- At the national level, we see corporations that have massive advertising budgets yet spend their advertising dollars with firms in which our people are not proportionately represented.
- There are others such as banks, credit unions, and other financial institutions that take our money, do nothing for the community and use our money to fund mortgages and business loans in other communities that they build and prosper with our money.
- Payday loan lenders are a particularly egregious lot. They loan money at high-interest rates and give nothing back to the community.
- Politicians are no exception. Many of them spend millions of dollars with white firms to get our vote and then turn around and ask us to volunteer.

The Philosophy of Strategic Economics as outlined here embraces the original idea of economics as *political economy*. So let's briefly look at the political economy to help us understand our approach to present-day economics.

Political Economy

It has been said that "[p]olitical economy is a branch of social science that studies the relationship that forms between a nation's population and its government when public policy is enacted. It is, therefore, the result of the interaction between politics and the economy and is the basis of the social science discipline."

In fact, political economy is the forerunner of modern-day

economics. It dealt with the relationship between the people, the government, and the policies of the government. Whether we like it or not, at the base of our problems in America we will always find the actions or inactions of the local and federal governments. When we recall that government policies are policies created by politicians that we put in office we will understand that it is partially by our own actions or inactions that we are oppressed.

Remember when we talk about policy, think *politics*. When we talk about economics in the United States we are invariably talking about *capitalism*.

Whether we like it or not we live in a capitalist society. Capitalism advocates profit as the motive force of advancement. Capitalists believe that private individuals and other actors, driven by their own (necessarily selfish) interests are best suited to benefit society as a whole. Put simply, capitalism is driven by self-interest and greed. The idea is that self-interest is the greatest motivator. But for capitalists the true goal, as they readily admit, is *profit*.

Profit is what is left over after expenses and taxes if any are paid - total revenue less total expenses. The profit in turn is reinvested or returned to shareholders in the form of dividends. *A dividend is money regularly paid to shareholders out of a company's profits. Shareholders are people who invest in the business with the expectation of dividends from profits in the future.*

What this really means, according to this view, is that private interest best serves societal advancement. That the bulk of advancement goes to benefit a small group of people seems by this view unimportant. But what is important for the purposes of our present analysis is that this capitalist profit/greed-driven approach gives economic power to a small group of people who in turn can affect political outcomes in their favor by the clever use of profits earned by their business and corporate activities.

*Please note that this is not intended to be a criticism of capitalism, although I could offer many, but only a statement of the reality that is the political/economic landscape in America today.*

Whether capitalism is the best economic system is beyond the scope of this writing, but it is the economic system in which we find ourselves. In order to be effective our strategies and tactics must be designed and implemented to accomplish our goals within the capitalist framework.

Going forward we must utilize the strategy of *Confrontational Politics* outlined above in everything we do because "power concedes nothing without a demand - it never did and it never will." This is why we have begun with Confrontational Politics and will now proceed to suggest economic strategies and tactics that if implemented will inevitably cause those who we target to change their behavior. Remembering always that political power is *the ability to take unilateral action in the face of the existence of actual or potential resistant force and to succeed in doing so. And also to prevent others from taking action that you consider undesirable in the face of actual or potential resistant force and to succeed in doing so.*

*Now let us look at how Strategic Economics will work.* Our plan for Strategic Economics envisions a three-pronged approach: (1) Reparations; (2) Strategic Lawsuits and (3) Direct Pressure. None of these is new. It is the combination of these launched by a non-partisan, non-profit, independent 501(c)(4) corporation that is unique.

Strategic Economics: Prong One: Reparations

**"We are coming to get our check!"
Dr. Martin Luther King, Jr.**

Introduction

Politics and economics are flip sides of the same coin. So, any attempt at Strategic Economics must start with what we are already owed - it's like money in the bank. Collecting debts, therefore, must be the first rule of Strategic Economics. My grandmother had a saying when we were kids that took me many years to understand. She said, "As long as I owe you, you'll never be broke." Technically, she was right, it's called accounts receivable. *Accounts receivables are considered assets subject to collection.*

In my humble view we, the descendants of enslaved Africans, are owed trillions of dollars in accounts receivable, that is, *assets subject to collection.*

My call for reparations did not just begin. In 1984, I was elected Chair of the National Black Law Students Association. I suggested our theme should be "1985-86 the Year of Compensation" and that the topic of our Frederick Douglass Moot Competition be a problem dealing with reparations. *I mention this to show that my call for reparations did not just begin. It began at least some 36 years ago in 1985. By way of comparison, the Late Rep. John Conyers introduced HR 40 for the first time in 1989. What follows is a verbatim excerpt from my campaign material dated March 20, 1985.*

"STRATEGY

"First, NBLSA should declare 1985-86 the "YEAR OF COMPENSATION." By so doing we commit our national prestige to the public debate of an issue that has been all but ignored since the days of the Freedmen's Bureau.

Second, the theme of the 18th Annual National Convention and General Assembly should be "COMPENSATION NOW!"

Third, this year's problem for the FREDERICK L. DOUGLASS MOOT COURT COMPETITION should be drawn hypothetically and should deal with a Black person or group, descended of American slaves, who seek compensation from the United States government for some 300 years of slavery in a suit at law or in equity. This will marshal the research ability of Black law students throughout the country. Further, by the use of judges and lawyers at all levels and in all states as competition judges, we will receive national insight on a subject that no court has passed upon.

Finally, the winning brief should be used as the seminal work from which to draft proposed legislation to be submitted to the CONGRESSIONAL Black CAUCUS to be introduced in Congress. The possibility of such legislation being passed is nil. Our objective, however, is not to pass legislation but to force discussion in public forums. Someone must take the initiative. No one is better suited to the task than NBLSA."

As you can see, I believed then, as I believe now, that we the descendants of the enslaved Africans are owed trillions of dollars in compensation and that we will never rest, and this country will never have peace until the debt is paid. What follows in my strategy to accomplish that end.

Unclaimed Property

Every state has an office of unclaimed property. It may be called by different names, but they all serve the same purpose. The law recognizes that people and corporations (also recognized as persons at law) should not keep money that belongs to another.

If for example your employer had wages for you, and you failed to claim them he cannot keep your wages even if he does not know how to contact you. After what is known as a dormancy period - usually one year the employer must submit the money to the government. It follows that slaveholders who did not pay wages should have been required to pay them into the state treasury against the day when the rightful owners or their descendants would claim them.

If you were owed those wages, would you not claim them? The question is rhetorical because the answer is obvious - of course, you would claim them. No matter how much it was. And if it is your money the government cannot withhold it because you might squander it. It is your money, and you may do with it as you please.

It follows that if we are owed compensation for the forced labor of our ancestors and for legislated discrimination thereafter, we must start by securing what is owed to us with interest. One very conservative estimate puts the figure at 1.5 million dollars per slave descendant. Others have placed the figure as high as 12-15 trillion dollars in the aggregate.

This amount is owed to the descendants of enslaved Africans who can be easily identified. This is because of African Americans who were in the United States prior to 1965 it is estimated that 90% were descendants of enslaved people.

Remember, if we let them, they will continue to have us running in place and going nowhere. Years, decades, centuries of commissions, studies, and meetings and always the same result. We must apply pressure. Whether reparations are owed is not a topic of discussion - *it is a fact. We are owed and we must be paid; this is non-negotiable.* The only thing that is negotiable is the amount we are owed. And even that is subject to only limited discussion. *We must not stop until we are paid.*

We must also recognize that the government will never give us reparations without a fight because *reparations are not about money, they are about power.* One of the specious arguments often made by white and Black opponents of reparations is that we would just squander the money and in no time, it would be gone and we would be back asking for a handout. The real objection, however, is the real fear that Black people with trillions of dollars at their disposal will use it to affect meaningful, substantive change that will benefit themselves and America at large. Reparations is not about money - the United States prints money - it is about power. They will not concede unless and until they are forced to. *Power concedes nothing without a demand.*

Unfortunately, reparations must be achieved politically. I say unfortunately because payment of the debt that is owed us by the United States government is controlled by politicians who control the government purse. No matter what they say, the reason they continue to withhold payment of an acknowl-edged and just debt is not about money but power.

The payment must be awarded by the United States Con-gress which means that 535 men and women are standing in the way of payment. Theoretically, the bill would come out of the appropriations committee (House and Senate). The bill would be to create a department of reparations whose responsibility would be to collect all data necessary to de-termine descendants of Africans enslaved in the United States by a date certain not to exceed twelve (12) months and to de-termine the amount owed to such descendants, with interest also to be determined by a date certain not to exceed twelve (12) months.

Digression: Japanese American Reparations

**"... when you see that you've got problems, all you have to do is examine the historic method used all over the world by others who have problems similar to yours. And once you see how they got theirs straight, then you know how you can get yours straight." Malcolm X**

With that instruction in mind let us look at how Japanese Americans campaigned for reparations and won.

In 1978, a group of Japanese Americans who belonged to the Japanese American Citizens League (JACL) started a full-court press for reparations for their internment during World War II. Ten years later and after the establishment of a com-mission to determine whether reparations were warranted, they got paid. There were people in the Japanese American community who were against reparations for various reasons. But that did not stop the JACL from pushing. They began to control the narrative through pressure on key politicians and their own members. They won the day by constant agitation and relentless demand.

Taking his lead from the success of the Japanese American community, the late Representative John Conyers introduced H.R. 40 in 1989. Thirty years later (2019) we had the first hearing on H.R. 40. It lasted 3 hours and did not call Dr. William A. Darity, Jr. ". . . perhaps the country's leading scholar on the economics of racial inequality." It appears that nothing has been done since. The bill was voted out of committee but has not been brought to the floor for debate. I still have not seen a committee report.

In the case of the descendants of enslaved Africans, the issue of reparations was acknowledged at the end of the Civil War by two indisputable facts:

First, General Sherman's Special Field Order #15 which confiscated 400,000 acres of land from Charleston, South Carolina to Jacksonville, Florida to be given to freedmen in 40-acre parcels. The Order, issued on January 16, 1865, had little lasting effect because President Lincoln was assassinated on April 15, 1865, and President Andrew Johnson, a Democrat, took office and proceeded to return the confiscated lands and pardon the rebels. Forty acres of land in South Carolina today is worth $704,400.00 ($17,610 per acre). In 1860 there were 412,320 slaves in South Carolina. You do the math. Let's just say it's a lot of money - in the trillions.

Second, the United States government made payments to slaveholders in the District of Columbia for the loss of their slave property. Payments were made at the set minimum amount of three hundred ($300.00) per slave. Since reparations must come from the United State government it is the government that must be forced to pay. That is done politically, A novel but not unprecedented idea is that the United States Government could seek indemnification from the states who held the slaves.

It must be the politicians who make it happen. Note also that the 13th, 14th, and 15th Amendments were only able to be passed because the rebel states were forced to go along to get back in the Union. This is why the only way it can be done is political. The method must be confrontational. Hence *Confrontational Politics. Constant agitation and relentless Demand (CARD).* We are owed and we must be paid. When we are paid, we won't need help from anyone. Think of it as if our money is being held as unclaimed property. Wages not paid to employees do not become the employers.

It should now be clear that politics and economics are closely related. In fact, they are flip sides of the same coin - the coin of power. Because this is true it follows that any plan of action must include both politics and economics.

Simply stated the problem is that we do not control our fair share of the resources of the country that we helped build. We worked and were not compensated. Those who we were forced to work for were handsomely compensated and as a result, were able to pass down massive generational wealth that explains the massive wealth gap between descendants of enslaved Africans and their enslavers today.

But the real problem is that we cannot wait 228 years to make up the deficit. We are owed depending on the estimate, upwards of $1.5 million dollars each. This amount is owed to the descendants of enslaved Africans who can be easily identified. It is estimated that of African Americans who were in the United States prior to 1965, 90% were descendants of enslaved people. What this indicates is that *our problem is both economic and political.* Economic because the descendants of African slaves are owed trillions of dollars and the only way we will be paid is if it becomes a political necessity. This means that we must be able to fight on more than one front.

Strategic Economics:
Prong Two: Strategic Lawsuits
The Equalization Strategy

We must recognize that many of our problems stem from discriminatory laws as well as discriminatory application of the laws. We must also recognize that an important tactic in our continuing battle against white supremacy has been and will continue to be a confrontation in the legal arena.

Many times, in our history it has been a lawsuit that has been used effectively to vindicate our rights. *Elmore v Rice and Brown vs Board of Education* immediately come to mind. I call it war in the courtroom. Lawsuits, however, are expensive and time-consuming. Not to mention that the present ultra-conservative courts including the United State Supreme Court are not only hostile to our attempts to pursue legal remedies but are also bent on turning back the clock on civil rights. See, *Shelby County v. Holder*, where the preclearance section of the 1965 Voting Rights Act was gutted.

We must not lose sight of what we are fighting for,

*power proportionality.* In South Carolina where 66.7% of the Democratic electorate is Black party elites have been able to maintain control and thwart the rising power of African Americans by secrecy, abuse of Robert's Rules of Order, rank interference with the internal affairs of county parties where Black people are in control; and rewarding those who are willing to look the other way.

Their strategy is simple and apparently effective: maintain control by dividing and conquering. Rewarding those who go along with crumbs from Massa's table and silencing those who do not. To be sure this is not a new tactic. In fact, it has been successfully used by both parties for decades.

The late Charles Hamilton Houston, Dean of Howard University Law School, the NAACP's first special counsel, and mentor of Thurgood Marshall who is often referred to as "the man who killed Jim Crow" developed what he called the "Equalization Strategy".

The Equalization Strategy was a plan of action formulated to counter the separate but equal legal doctrine established in *Plessy v. Ferguson* in 1896. It was this legal strategy that, in the end, made racial segregation in public primary and secondary schools unconstitutional. We must implement an equalization strategy of our own if we are to accomplish similar goals and outcomes in the economic arena.

In short, the equalization strategy was a plan of action that has been called a "stroke of genius". This legal strategy was to end school segregation by *defeating the lie* that facilities for Black students though separate when they existed at all, were demonstrably not equal to those provided to white students as a matter of law.

Mr. Houston's strategy was to expose the lie that was separate but equal. In our quest for compensation, we must expose the multi-faceted lie that says that we are not due reparations and that even if we are the descendants of enslaved Africans cannot be identified. This is a lie, and we must expose it.

Strategic Economics:

Prong Three: Direct Pressure

Introduction

Let's face it. Collectively we handle a lot of money - 1.2 trillion dollars *annually*. But we don't spend it strategically. We support those who disrespect us. Alfred Edmond Jr., Editor-at-large of Black Enterprise magazine has observed that:

"To the degree, we withhold our spending from companies that are harmful, disrespectful, or unfair to Black consumers, and intentionally direct our dollars toward companies (including Black-owned businesses) that are beneficial to Black communities and value Black consumers, our spending power is important."

We should think twice about supporting businesses that establish themselves in our neighborhoods but give nothing back to the community. This is only common sense.

In 1941, Adam Clayton Powell, Jr., perhaps the single most effective Black politician in history started an effective boycott, perhaps the first based on the notion that we should not shop where we can't work. In the 1940's Black folk could ride the buses but were not being hired as drivers. Adam's boycott lasted four weeks and resulted in the hiring of 200 bus drivers and mechanics.  He also boycotted stores on 125th Street in Harlem that would hire us as janitors but not salespersons.

Today we have stores all over the country, particularly in Black neighborhoods that do not hire Black folk yet derive virtually their entire revenue from Black folk in the surrounding neighborhoods.  We are in this sense *targeted*. This must stop.

Some say these businesses should not have to hire or support the communities from which they derive their income. But that is not their (the business') decision.  It must be a requirement for our support of their business.  They can open the store, but we don't have to buy from them.  We must develop a way to acknowledge and support businesses that meet standards we have determined are necessary for us to reward them with our support.

Our ability to generate community and generational wealth is dependent upon our ability to control our spending for both essentials and non-essentials.  Our ability to control essentials such as rent/mortgages and taxes is limited but our ability to control where we spend our money for other essentials such as food, clothing, and all non-essentials can be controlled. *Politics and economics flip sides of the coin of power*

It should now be clear that politics and economics are closely related.  In fact, they are the flip sides of the coin of power.  Because this is true it follows that any plan of action must include both politics and economics.  Hence, the necessity for *strategic economics.*

Whether we like it or not we live in a capitalist society.  Capitalism advocates profit as the motive force of advancement.

Capitalists believe that private individuals and other actors, driven by their own (necessarily selfish) interests are best suited to benefit society as a whole. Put simply, capitalism is driven by self-interest and greed. The idea is that self-interest is the greatest motivator. But for capitalists the true goal, as they readily admit, is *profit*. Profit is what is left over after expenses and taxes are paid - total revenue less total expenses. The profit in turn is reinvested or returned to shareholders in the form of dividends.

*A dividend is money regularly paid to shareholders out of a company's profits. Shareholders are people who invest in the business with the expectation of dividends from profits in the future.*

What this really means, according to this view, is that private interest best serves societal advancement. That the bulk of advancement goes to benefit a small group of people seems by this view unimportant. But what is important for the purposes of our present analysis is that this capitalist profit/greed-driven approach gives economic power to a small group of people who in turn can affect political outcomes in their favor by the clever use of profits earned by their business and corporate activities. *Please note that this is not intended to be a criticism of capitalism but only a statement of the reality that is the political/economic landscape in America today.*

Protest Divestment

What would happen if we began to think of ourselves as *shareholders* in businesses that we spend money with? First, it would mean that we are entitled to dividends from profits.

Second, it means that as shareholders we have the right to be heard on matters affecting the corporation. Third, we have the right to *disinvest*.

To my knowledge, this is a unique approach to dealing with problems that have confronted us for decades if not centuries. It has always been that since we did not own the businesses in our communities that we were seen merely as consumers whose job it is to *consume*. It was not our job to do anything but buy, often at exorbitant prices and go home. After all, what else could we do? This again is a problem in our thinking. Strategic economics dictate that we see ourselves for what we are. Our patronage of any business, particularly those in our communities is in effect the equivalent of purchasing shares in those businesses which makes us *shareholders*. And as shareholders, we are entitled to dividends or to disinvest. By disinvestment, we mean taking our funds out of the corporation.

You may remember that one of the effective strategies that assisted in the dismantling of Apartheid in South Africa was the Protest Disinvestment Movement largely started by students on United States college campuses. This form of dissent can be used successfully in our communities and nationally if we recognize that businesses cannot survive without our investment and even those that can would rather have our dollars than not have them because in many cases they represent a significant portion of their bottom line. To complete our understanding of Strategic Economics we must understand the important distinction between disposable and discretionary income.

Digression: Disposable vs Discretionary Income

For individuals (you and I) the equivalent of profit is the difference in *disposable income* and *discretionary income.* *Disposable income* is money left over from salary after taxes. *Discretionary income* is what is left of disposable income after paying for necessities: rent, mortgage, health, etc. that is, money that can be spent on *non-essentials.* Discretionary income then is the amount of income left over after we have taken care of essentials. It is the same as profit to a corporation. And like a corporation it can be reinvested or paid to the shareholder - *you.*

Let's face it. We collectively handle a lot of money. 1.2 trillion dollars annually. That is a lot of money. But we don't spend it strategically. We support those who disrespect us by spending our money with them. We support businesses that open in our neighborhoods but give nothing back to our community - not even a job. Some say they should not have to. But they should have to if it is a requirement for our support. You can open the store but we don't have to buy from you.

For example, after taxes and necessities, we spend our discretionary income on things that have no lasting value. We spend over $800 million on hair products, and toiletries, including soap and bath needs. And another $800 million on bottled water. We also spend more than 50% of all dollars spent on dry vegetables and grain ($473.3M); 42% of baby food ($817M); 41% of personal soap and bath needs ($1.3B); 38% of fresheners and deodorizers ($774.1M); and shelf stable juices and drinks ($2.3B). This is where most of our discretionary income goes. Put another way, we are taking our profit and investing it in businesses that do not pay dividends. Suppose we pledged to cut those expenses in half and invest that money? More importantly, we could force the companies that we purchase these items from to invest in our communities, that is, *pay dividends*. Or we stop buying their products altogether - *disinvest.* Disinvestment is simply a fancy word for no dividends no investment. This is *strategic economics.*

Strategic Economics: Tactical Ideas

We must develop a way to acknowledge and support businesses that meet standards we have determined are necessary for us to reward them with our support. A recognized seal of approval can be provided to those businesses that meet or exceed the standard. Something similar to the UL Seal of Approval. Underwriters Laboratories, Inc., does not endorse any product. Their seal simply means they have tested the product and it met or exceeded their safety standards. We will create our own standards.

Another tactic would be to fund businesses providing the same services in nearby locations to give our people an alternative to businesses that do not meet the standard. If a store is in our community is a successful business (because we spend money with them) that means that an opportunity exists for a Black business providing the same product or service - that will meet our standards. No need to reinvent the wheel.

Our targets must be those businesses and other entities that derive a significant portion of their annual revenue from the Black community. Companies that we support should be willing to support us.  By that I mean they should be willing to put their money where their mouth is. It is not enough to advertise that you support us, put the money where it will do the most good. Support us by supporting *us!*

Tactics: The Power of the Strategic Boycott

Boycotts are not new.  A boycott is simply a refusal (individual or collective) to spend money or do business with any entity that does not live up to your standards. It is very often used to achieve ends and for political reasons.

In 1941, Adam Clayton Powell, Jr., perhaps the single most effective Black politician in history started an effective boycott, perhaps the first based on the notion that we should not shop where we can't work.  In the 1940's Black folk could ride the buses but were not being hired.  Adam's boycott lasted four weeks and resulted in the hiring of 200 bus drivers and mechanics.  He also boycotted stores on 125th Street in Harlem that would hire us as janitors but not salespersons.

In order to be effective boycotts must be used strategically. That is they must be targeted and focused to stop a problem by calling attention to it.  But the main intention of the successful boycott must be to demonstrate the intention of a people to control their one destiny and to demonstrate their recognition of the power they possess. Businesses already recognize your power each time they look at their bottom line. They recognize your power when they plan their advertising budgets.  They recognize your power when they fund research and development. And they recognize your power when they contribute to political campaigns and political PACs.   But as long as you do not recognize the power you possess, they will go on ignoring you and laughing all the way to the bank because you buy their products and services without their having to do anything.  From their standpoint, if it ain't broke don't fix it. Remember it is always the noisy wheel that gets the oil. *Constant agitation and relentless demand.*

## CHAPTER ELEVEN

# Political Partisanship

*"A vote for a Democrat is a vote for a Dixiecrat . . . .*
*it's time now for you and me to become more*
*politically mature and realize what the*
*ballot is for; what we're supposed to get*
*when we cast a ballot;" Malcolm X*

*No Party or Politician Should Be*
*Allowed to Take Us For Granted - Ever Again.*

As is often the case, history is our best teacher. We must look at the history of our support of the two major political parties and learn from their historical actions to understand their actions today. The two major parties have both used us and abandoned us. Each promised to support us in return for our vote. Each time we have fallen for their promises and each time we have been deceived. *History is our best teacher.*

From its founding the Democratic Party has been alternately the party of slavery, the Black Codes, Jim Crow, segregation, and voter suppression. The Radical wing of the Republican Party advocated for us in an attempt to break the economic power of the Democratic Party in the South and not, contrary to popular misinformation, for our freedom although the Thirteenth, Fourteenth, and Fifteenth Amendments were a result of those efforts. To be clear had slavery not been such an important part of the wealth and power of the South emancipation might not have come.

As a result of the Civil War the South was rendered destitute both economically and politically. Much of its infrastructure had been demolished. It would have to be rebuilt. Although the rebels had been pardoned and allowed to keep their guns they had no slaves to do the work for them. The rebels lost the war but never conceded defeat. The only way to rebuild was through a program of reconstruction. But the workers, mostly former slaves, were now at least theoretically, free agents. But they were for the most part unarmed and at the mercy of those who had held them in bondage. In short, they had no guns and no way to protect themselves. They had no resources, no power and no enforcement mechanism. The success of Reconstruction, therefore, depended on the presence of Federal troops to protect the former slaves from being re-enslaved in all but name.

The election of 1876 resulted in the Compromise of 1877. The Republicans, no longer radical but no less racist, bargained our freedom for their political control. The Compromise of 1877 had several very important consequences: (1) Rutherford B. Hayes became the president; (2) the removal of Federal troops from the South; and (3) the passage of the Black Codes and segregation. By far the most important of these was the removal of Federal troops which left the formerly enslaved unprotected and put Reconstruction under the control of Southern Governors and legislators.

We see from this that both Democrats and Republicans have promised to support us and abandoned us after the election. There is an old saying "Fool me once shame on you, fool me twice shame on me". How long will we continue to believe demonstrated deceivers?

We Must Follow Interest Not Party

Digression: Dissociative Behavior

Let us imagine that a person who is responsible for the care and protection of another individual is confronted with the following scenario:

The person (let us call him/her the Protector) witnesses the physical abuse of the person (let us call him/her the Protected) to whom the Protector owes the duty of protection. The Protector's first instinct is to spring to the defense of the Protected by taking affirmative action to stop the physical abuse, violently, aggressively and immediately. But, despite his/her first instinct he/she does nothing. He fails to act as if his very ability to act has been paralyzed. Perhaps more importantly, he does not find his failure to act unjustified.

On the other and instinctive level, however, her failure to act is irrational and counterproductive. It is as if he has two minds counseling diametrically opposed actions simultaneously. The conflict lies in the fact that instinct informs the Protector that he/she must take immediate action to insure the survival of the Protected. This is instinct—this is survival technology at its life-sustaining best. This is survival technology operating to insure protection defensively, and collectively.

The conscious mind, however, is heavily influenced by the belief system upon which it must necessarily rely to make decisions, to plan and counsel. The belief system includes beliefs about life and death. The conscious mind may have concluded that the aggressor in the scenario is too big, too strong, or that he has a gun, or that there are too many of them—the Protector could suffer bodily injury or worse, he/she could get killed.

To the conscious mind what is right, what is required is to do nothing because to act may mean death. The right thing to do is to avoid even the possibility of death by doing nothing. At the instinctive level, however, the Protector has only one concern—survival. At all costs, and to the exclusion of all things, protect and defend so the *genus* survives.

Of course, this is also why the fear of death is not instinctive. The fear of death is learned and incorporated in our belief system. If the fear of death were instinctive it would defeat or neutralize the innate instinct to survive. We should also note here, in passing, that this is precisely why self-preservation cannot be the first law of nature. It is the *genus*, the group, the *genus* that must be preserved, not the individual. It is of course true that the *genus* cannot survive unless the individuals who comprise it survive. But, self-preservation cannot possibly be the main focus of survival. The survival of the individual means nothing in the wider context of the continuation of life.

Let us say that an individual adopts the self-preservation rule. Let us also say that he/she adheres to the rule religiously. What is the result? We have a person who, no matter what, will insure his/her own survival. This necessarily means that he/she will be forced to choose between his preservation and that of his family, clan, tribe or nation. His/her only concern is his or herself. In the worst case scenario the survival of me ensures that I live, but I cannot reproduce alone. What I have accomplished then is that I will have the dubious distinction of being the last one of my line. *I have lived to become extinct.*

This is not clear thinking. This is evidence of a highly detrimental mind-set that was foisted upon us and that we have now unwittingly adopted in the centuries since our initial imprisonment in America.

The point here is that we must start acting in our own interest. We must not buy into the notion that we must do what is best for America. We are Americans by birth but we have always been treated like foreigners and aliens. We have never been part of the fabric of America; the melting pot concept is a myth and a rising tide cannot lift the boat that you do not have. The only thing it will do is eventually drown you. The dubious and apparently tentative gains that we have achieved have only come after generations of constant agitation and relentless demand.

Even when we were legally recognized as citizens the forces of white supremacy have done everything possible to prevent us from securing the rights of citizenship. And now more than 150 years after the passage of the 14th Amendment we are watching the renewed attempt to turn back the clock. We have tried at every turn to embrace American ideals and the promises of freedom, justice and equality. But we can no longer ignore the fact that we must act in our collective interests. We must recognize that the system that enslaved us was not designed to free us.

*History is our best teacher.* We know from the treatment of Native Americans that the promises of the American government are worthless, and their treaties are not worth the paper they were written on. We still await our 40 acres and the mule. History teaches us that they will sell us out no matter what they promise. That is the nature of politics and the misfortune of people who do not effectively use their power. Let's face it. The promises of both parties are worthless. President Biden has promised criminal justice reform but was the author of the Violent Crime Control and Law Enforcement Act of 1994 and co-sponsor of the Anti-Drug Abuse Act of 1986. President Clinton signed the 1994 Crime Bill that Biden authored. The Anti-Drug Abuse Act was introduced by a Democrat (Jim Wright D-TX) and signed into law by Republican President Ronald Reagan. And co sponsored by a host of Black Democratic representative and Senators

We have to remember that our job is to look out for each other. We are family. Because the bottom line is all people take care of their families. We are the only ones who will sell our people out for an extra crust of bread when if we band together we all survive and prosper. Why? because our portion of the wealth of this nation should always be at least proportionate to our numbers in the population. Anything less and we and our children are being robbed.

## Our Declaration of Independence
## We Must Be Independent

It now seems clear that an independence movement of sorts is taking place in the United States. According to a 2021 Gallup Poll, 42% of Americans are independents. "Overall, in 2021, an average of 29% of Americans identified as Democrats, 27% as Republicans, and 42% as independents. Apparently, independents now represent the largest voting bloc in America. We, that is African Americans, must become part of this necessary trend away from parties - not away from the vote. We cannot continue to allow the Democratic Party or the Republican Party to control our votes.

A few years back Oprah Winfrey stated the argument best when she said she was a registered independent because she didn't want any party telling her what decisions she gets to make for herself. Nor should we.

I'm not sure how many people are aware of it but the Declaration of Independence is not an organic document of the United States. It is a bunch of pretty, high-sounding words that have absolutely no authority over anything. It is not a law, ordinance, or treaty. There is a reason for that. The Declaration of Independence declared the right of the people to revolt. Apparently, that right could only be exercised by white men who had grievances against other white men. Once the revolution was over not even white men had the right to revolt. This is just as well since we, I mean Black folk, were not included or even considered part of the hypocritical uproar over freedom. Yes, I said hypocritical. There is one thing it is

THE POWER WE POSSESS – 95

good for and that gives it more value than the parchment it was written on. *It can be a powerful tool when used to inspire.*

We African Americans were never included in the Declaration of independence and were, in fact left out because slavery belies its pretensions and hypocritical claims particularly that all men are created equal and endowed by their creator with certain inalienable rights among these are life, liberty and the pursuit of happiness - in less grandiose terms the right to be free! Despite its palpable hypocrisy it still lays a philosophical groundwork from which to inspire us to the next level in our struggle.

Now that I have some readers scared - sit back -take a deep breath. I do not mean that we should declare independence from the United States government. I mean that we must declare independence from blind allegiance to political parties starting with the Democratic Party. In short, we must declare ourselves independent *en masse.*

I know that for some people this tactic will seem counterproductive and perhaps even counterintuitive. The argument goes that Republicans don't want us and Democrats take us for granted. The fact of the matter is that the Republicans see us as a lost cause (as in lost to the Democrats) while Democrats have become fat and lazy off our votes. They fully anticipate that we will remain on their plantation no matter what. This notion is reinforced by the simple fact that the same tactics used on the plantation still work today. Can you blame them? As the old saying goes "If it ain't broke don't fix it!"

*Plantation Politics*

It is interesting to me that there is so much contro-
versy about the term "plantation politics" given America's
centuries-long history of the maintenance of plantations and
slavery.

Lest we forget: The Democratic Party was the party of
slavery, the Black Codes, Jim Crow, and segregation. Plantation owners in the antebellum South were almost exclusively
Democrats. That they were able to maintain slavery so effi-
ciently that they created a booming economy that was based
on slave labor and which was collateralized not by their produce but by their ownership of slaves.

It seems too obvious to note that in order to maintain
their economy they had to be able to control their enslaved
people. That they had to have methods and practices per-
fected over time to produce maximum productivity while at
the same time holding human beings - the manufacturers of
their wealth, captive and productive.

So, they cannot now be heard to decry the argument that
similar tactics are being utilized to maintain political control
and productivity of descendants of those who were held captive. The analogy is clearly appropriate.

For the record plantation politics is here defined as the
use of strategies and tactics by political parties to maintain
political allegiance similar to the strategies and tactics used
on plantations to control enslaved people in the antebellum
South. Period. That the argument may make some people

uncomfortable is unfortunate. It does not, however, undermine the analogy or the appropriateness of its use.

It is true that the argument is most often used by Republicans to describe the continuing support of the Democratic
Party by African Americans. It is often described as our being
stuck on the *Democrat plantation.* Part of the argument is that
our minds are controlled by the Democratic Party. Meaning
that we are incapable of thinking for ourselves. This notion
is insulting. It is not that we cannot think for ourselves. But
rather that we are pragmatists, and the Democratic Party is
the lesser of two evils (maybe). A pragmatist is "someone who
deals with problems in a sensible way that suits the conditions
that really exist, rather than following fixed theories, ideas,
or rules."

We went with Republicans because Abraham Lincoln was
a Republican and the Republicans pushed through the 13th,
14th, and 15th Amendments; we went with Democrats because Franklin Delano Roosevelt was a Democrat who promised a New Deal. Our choices were always pragmatic.

The pragmatic approach dictates that we look at our problems in a sensible way that suits the conditions as they really
exist and without regard to the rules that have been dictated
to us by others. We are now a power to be reckoned with and
not ignored so long as our vote is needed for anyone to win.
To the extent any party can accurately predict what we will do,
that party can take us for granted or ignore us completely.

Democrats take us for granted because they know that
85-87% of us will vote for them. Republicans ignore us because they know that on the best day only 6-8% will vote for

them. In short, Democrats take us for granted and Republicans don't care.

So, what tactics similar to those used on plantations to keep enslaved people in line are still being used today? It is no secret that George Washington the first President was a slaveholder. Nor is it a secret that he signed the first Fugitive Slave Act in 1793. When he died in 1799, there were 317 enslaved people at the Mount Vernon plantation. President Washington employed tactics similar to those used by plantation owners to control their slaves generally. Of course, whippings and other forms of physical punishment were employed. Clearly, these cannot be employed today, except by modern-day equivalents of the antebellum slave patrols now known as the police. But other tactics are still employed by the Democratic *and* Republican parties.

**"In addition to having overseers monitoring work on site, George Washington utilized a number of methods to try to control the labor and behavior of the Mount Vernon slaves. Since work as a house servant or skilled laborer was viewed as higher-ranking than fieldwork, Washington could threaten to demote an artisan who would be punished by becoming a field worker." and, "Washington occasionally tried to encourage an individual's pride as motivation. In addition to verbal encouragement, material incentives were attempted as well. Finer quality blankets and clothing were given out to those slaves who were considered to be "most deserving. "Direct cash rewards were also given out to slaves as a means of encouragement."**

Sound familiar? Political parties use the same tactics

today - fear of economic or other forms of retaliation such as demotion or ostracism within the party for those who speak out and promotion or direct cash payments to those who tow the party line. *Just like on the plantation*. Instead of trying to get off the plantation, we are trying to get in the Big House not recognizing that even if we get into the Big House, we will still be slaves.

It's time for a change. From this day forward no party should be able to count on our vote unless it meets our demands. Remember there will be few elections where our collective vote can be ignored. They will come to us because they will have no choice.

One of the ongoing problems within the Democratic Party is how to attract younger voters to its ranks. Part of the reason is young people are saying "... we don't want to be in a party, we are independents and we want to do politics in a new way'." It does not take a rocket scientist to recognize that independents may be the wave of the future. We must be part of that wave. *A Black independent wave.* More than any people in America we should be independent from party control. I say this because no people have consistently supported parties, whether Democratic or Republican, than African Americans. And no people have been more consistently disappointed by both.

*We owe no allegiance to any party.* Any party that we have supported has reaped far more rewards than we have. Such that any debt owed to any party has been paid many times over. *We are still waiting for ours.*

*We Can Use Our Vote to Elect or Defeat*

I have often been told how important my vote is. I have been repeatedly urged that I must vote because my vote could be the deciding one. I was also told horror stories about how our ancestors gave their lives for the right to vote. Admittedly, I have been guilty of using the same argument to get others, particularly young people to vote with the mantra that every vote counts. But the fact of the matter is that *it is not our individual vote but our collective vote that counts.* We often hear people say that we are not a monolith. Whether that is true or not (the jury is still out on that one) we must be monolithic in politics. By monolithic I mean we must vote as one. We can not allow them to continue to split our vote. This is no more than the ancient military strategy of divide and conquer. Just for the record a monolith is defined as a "large and Impersonal political, corporate, or social structure regarded as intractably indivisible and uniform."

To the extent that we do become monolithic in politics we can elect or defeat any candidate who does not support our issues and concerns. We can start this process by a simple tactic. When called upon to answer surveys say you are *independent.* In states where you have to declare a party declare as independent rather than Democrat or Republican or any other party. We are taken for granted because we are *predictable*. Predictable creatures are the easiest prey whether two or four legged. We outsmart animals because they are predictable. This is particularly true of politics. We must learn to keep our enemies guessing. We could determine the outcome of most elections if we kept them guessing. We have said war is about confusion and deception. *KEEP THEM GUESSING!* They should never be sure of how we will vote - only that we will vote and as a block.

## *We Must Form Supportive Alliances*
### *"The enemy's enemy is my friend." Sun Tzu*

We cannot forget that we must have allies in order to effect real, substantive change. This means that we can and should ally ourselves with any group that supports our interests or whose interests are not adverse to ours. For example, a particular group is noncommittal on the issue of reparations. But they are supportive of substantive criminal justice reform. Is alliance possible? I think so because criminal justice reform is one of our issues. Let's look at another. We cannot vote for a Democrat such as George Wallace but do we vote for a Republican like Romney in order to defeat Wallace? There is no right or wrong answer. The issue is whether we are interested in making the best of all situations or whether we want to remain second-class citizens living in the shadow of political party elites whether Black or white, Democrat or Republican. We must forge alliances whenever, wherever, and with whoever serves our interests.

### *"America has no permanent friends or enemies, only interests." Henry Kissinger.*

*Likewise, we must have no permanent friends, and no permanent enemies, only our self-identified permanent interests.*

## Conclusion

The question we began with was why African Americans, Black folk, have not attained political power in America at least proportionate to our numbers in the population. The answer we said was our collective failure to develop effective political strategies and tactics. But at first, we must, at all costs, recognize, understand and acknowledge that we are at war. Because unless and until we do so we will continue to be slaves to the pernicious system of white supremacy.

I refer throughout this essay to the "enemy". I conclude by reiterating that the enemy is not white people but the ideology of white supremacy that although created and advanced by white males the real enemy against which we must do battle is a political, economic, and cultural ideology. White supremacy is an all-encompassing strategy designed to ensure that certain people rule the world in perpetuity. *It is made up of an intricate series of interlocking laws, policies, treaties, and judicial opinions based on custom and usage and backed by the ever-present threat of massive violent force.*

The foregoing then is a blueprint for real, substantive change. But it will not change a thing unless it is fiercely and effectively implemented. We must begin with the Critical Mass. If you have read this book and agree you are one of the gifted people who have connected the dots and seen that we are at war, and you have a burning desire to take action now! You are not alone.

We need only to make contact with our brothers and sisters who have reached the level of enriched consciousness and *organize, organize, organize*. The time is right - everything is falling into place. One report has found that "Ninety-six percent of African Americans own a smartphone, and those aged 35+ surpass the total population in their age group by 2% for smartphone ownership. In fact, African Americans make up 23% of the total market for U.S. cellular sales, while only accounting for 14% of the overall population."

Let us remember and be inspired by the immortal words of Frederick Douglass:

*"Power concedes nothing without a demand. It never did and it never will. find out just what any people will quietly submit to and you have found out the exact measure of injustice and wrong which will be imposed upon them, and these will continue till they are resisted with either words or blows, or with both. The limits of tyrants are prescribed by the endurance of those whom they oppress."*

DO YOU KNOW WHAT POWER *YOU* POSSESS?

# Notes

CHAPTER ONE

1. ˆ The Voting Rights Act of 1965 at 50: How It Changed the World | Time.
2. ˆ The Hidden Holocaust: How King Leopold II Murdered 10 Million Africans. | The African Exponent. 1514–1866,
3. ˆThe Transatlantic Slave Trade | National Museum of African American History & Culture. (searchablemuseum.com)
4. ˆ DEATH TOLL FROM THE SLAVE TRADE (worldfuture-fund.org)
5. ^Kmt, Kemet 'Egypt' : its etymology (July 7, 2021) (nofi.media) The name ancient Egyptians called themselves meaning "The black one." Or the land of the Blacks?
6. ˆ The Berlin Conference of 1884-1885 | Africa's Great Civilizations | PBS LearningMedia
7.

8. CHAPTER TWO

9. Old High German werran, German verwirren "to confuse, perplex"), said in Watkins to be from PIE *wers- (1) "to confuse, mix up," suggesting
10. the original sense was "bring into confusion."
11.

12. CHAPTER THREE

13. ˆB2B2367 Tactical Planning.pdf (marines.mil)
14. ˆword usage - Origin of the term White Supremacy? - English Language & Usage Stack Exchange
15. ˆNew York, 1868] by John H. Van Evrie, M.D. Van Evrie, Horton & Co.

16. ^"New Division of the Earth by the Different Species or 'Races' of Man that Inhabit It"
17. ^Greed Definition & Meaning - Merriam-Webster
18. ^ Facts About the U.S. Black Population | Pew Research Center
19. ^How to Understand Urban Blight in America's Neighborhoods and Work to Eliminate It | Dickinson College
20. ^Inequality in Public School Funding | American University
21. ^ Is It Time to Stop Funding Schools With Local Property Taxes? – Ed Note (ecs.org)
22. ^1 Official Proceedings of the Constitutional Convention of the State of Alabama, May 21st 1901 to September 3rd, 1901, p. 8 1940. Cited in Hunter v. Underwood, 471 U.S. 222 (1985)
23. ^471 U.S. 222 (1985)
24. ^ Disenfranchise Definition & Meaning - Merriam-Webster
25. ^ The Average Black Family Would Need 228 Years to Build the Wealth of a White Family Today
26. ^ scholarlycommons.law.wlu.edu/cgi/viewcontent.cgi?article=4244&context=w
27. ^ "Some modern translations word this as "servants" but that is dishonest because the original text is about owned slaves, not paid servants." Cline, Austin. "Tenth Commandment: Thou Shalt Not Covet." Learn Religions, Feb. 8, 2021, learnreligions.com/tenth-commandment-thou-shalt-not-covet-250909.
28. ^ The Decline of the Lawyer-Politician (buffalo.edu)
29. ^ Disciplinary Power and Consumer Research: an Introduction | ACR (acrwebsite.org)
    *Power and energy are synonymous terms and are here used interchangeably.

CHAPTER FIVE

30. ^ Introduction to Politics | Law, Politics, and Philosophy (wordpress.com)
31. ^ economic warfare | international law | Britannica
32. ^ Strategy Definition & Meaning - Merriam-Webster
33. ^ economics - Search (bing.com)
34. ^ Political Economy Definition (investopedia.com)
35. ^ Calculating Reparations: $1.5 Million for Each Slave Descendant in the U.S | Black Agenda Report

36.    ˆ How Japanese Americans Campaigned For Reparations—And Won : Code Switch : NPR

37.    ˆ H.R.40 - Commission to Study and Develop Reparation Proposals for African-Americans Act 116th Congress (2019-2020)

38.    ˆ Can Progressives Be Convinced That Genetics Matters? | The New Yorker

39.    ˆ (1865) General William T. Sherman's Special Field Order No. 15 • (blackpast.org)

40.    ˆ Andrew Johnson | The White House

41.    ˆ     https://www.zippia.com/wp-content/uploads/2021/07/average-acre-land-costs-each-state.png

42.    ˆ South Carolina - African-Americans - Slave Population (sciway.net)

43.    ˆ The District of Columbia Emancipation Act | National Archives

44.    ˆ *Elmore V.Rice,72 F,Supp.(E.D.S.C 1047) ; Rice v. Elmore, 165 F.2d 387 (1947)*

45.    ˆ *Brown v. Board of Education of Topeka, 347 U.S. 483 (1954),*

46.    ˆ *Shelby County v. Holder, 570 U.S. 529 (2013)*

47.    ˆ 163 U.S. 537 (1896)

48.    ˆ Black Buying Power Is Not A Measure of Real Wealth (blackenterprise.com)

49.    ˆ "Don't Buy Where You Can't Work" Sounds Familiar (dailykos.com)

50.    ˆ "Protest divestment is a form of dissent in which stockholders intentionally sell their assets from a corporation to enact social change. By selling off stocks, protesters hope to influence corporations against performing some aspect of their business.

   In this case, those opposed to apartheid wanted to keep companies from doing business in South Africa."

51.    ˆ Black Impact: Consumer Categories Where African Americans Move Markets – Nielsen. See also, The Black consumer: A $300 billion opportunity | McKinsey

52. Id.                                                      CHAPTER ELEVEN

   53. "Don't Buy Where You Can't Work" Sounds Familiar (dailykos.com)

54.    ˆ H.R.3355 - 103rd Congress (1993-1994): Violent Crime

Control and Law Enforcement Act of 1994 | Congress.gov | Library of Congress

55.  ^ H.R.5484 - Anti-Drug Abuse Act of 1986 99th Congress ... https://www.congress.gov/bill/99th-congress/house-bill/5484

56.  ^ U.S. Political Party Preferences Shifted Greatly During 2021 (gallup.com)

57.  ^ Oprah Winfrey - Why I'm an Independent Voter - Independent Voting

58.  ^ It's not just Latinos and younger voters. Democrats are slipping among Black voters too. (msn.com)

59.  ^ Ten Facts About Washington & Slavery · George Washington's Mount Vernon

60.  ^ Slave Control · George Washington's Mount Vernon

61.  ^ Black America | Independent Voting

62.  ^ Alabama Governor from 1963 -1967, who in September 1963, attempted to stop four black students from enrolling in four separate elementary schools in Huntsville. After intervention by a federal court in Birmingham, the four children were allowed to enter on September 9, becoming the first to integrate a primary or secondary school in Alabama. Wallace's most infamous and telling quote was

" . . . *segregation now, segregation tomorrow, segregation forever.*"

Dr. Johnnie Cordero, B.A., J.D., holds a bachelor's degree in political science and a doctorate in jurisprudence. He is the President and CEO of the South Carolina Community Black Caucus a 501 (c)(4) nonprofit organization and host of *"The Cordero Report" Podcast.* He is also a frequent political contributor and commentator for The Minority Eye and author of three prior works entitled: *"Total Black Empowerment Through the Creation of Powerful Minds: A Mind Primer for the Twenty-First Century and Beyond"* © 2007; *"Total Black Empowerment: A Guide to Critical Thinking in The Age of Trump."* © 2017; and *"Theodicy and The Power of The African Will: A Prognostication Based on The Wisdom of Our Ancient African Ancestors."*© 2017. He was born in Brooklyn, New York and now lives in Columbia, South Carolina.

www.ingramcontent.com/pod-product-compliance
Lightning Source LLC
Chambersburg PA
CBHW071237020426
42333CB00015B/1507